Magical Window Stars

Frédérique Guéret

Magical Window Stars

Floris Books

Translated by Anna Cardwell

Drawings: Frédérique Guéret
Photos: Louis Marie Guéret

First published in German in 2005 under the title
Leuchtende Fenstersterne — Transparente aus Seidenpapier
by Verlag Freies Geistesleben
First published in English by Floris Books in 2005
Fourth printing 2015

British Library CIP Data available
ISBN 978-086315-494-2

Printed in China

Contents

Introduction

Beautiful tissue paper transparencies give an exciting, almost mysterious touch to your window. The colours and the strong forms attract the eye like magic. After initial astonishment, the beholder then feels admiration. The harmonious unity created between form and colour make it difficult to imagine that these transitory works of art are made up of single folded sheets. Perhaps the question will arise how such a small, delicate marvel is made.

Sunlight streaming through the window causes a fascinating interplay of lines and texture. And there are always new aspects of these luminous colourful ornaments to be found, as the fine geometric lines penetrate each other continuously. It can indeed appear as if some of the transparencies are able to move even though they are fixed to the window. Tissue paper transparencies stimulate the creative fantasy of the observer. Is it a sparkling star rising on the horizon? Is it the sun's ball rotating slowly as it radiates warmth? Now it is a cold blue snowflake. Or is it a blossom being carried away by the wind? Often a dainty star shines through a cut crystal. Or a flower reveals itself in the heart of a sun. There are numerous possibilities. The four seasons are reflected artistically in the play of light through the transparencies.

The joy of this creative and contemplative art of folding starts with the first rustling of tissue paper. Step-by-step instructions guide you through the folding process, the clear figures only seemingly complicated. Each transparency is interesting to fold. Exact folding and a calm state of mind will lead to satisfactory results.

This new book offers a range of designs, created mainly out of basic rectangular sheets of tissue paper. You can vary the models and make up your own, to expand and enrich the creative possibilities of the art of folding.

As well as valuable practical experience gained by folding the tissue paper there are also therapeutic aspects to this art. The calming or stimulating effects of harmonious colours are in addition to the ornamental value of these transparencies and can help create a healing focus of joy and energy.

May these new transparencies accompany you throughout the year and the corresponding seasonal festivals and awaken enthusiasm in visitors and friends.

Materials

You will not need much material to make these impressive coloured tissue paper creations.

Tissue paper is sold in large sheets, either singly or as a set, usually in a standard size of 20 × 30 inches in North America, and 50 cm × 70 cm in Britain and Europe. If using American paper size, shorten the sheet to 28 in exactly. In the instructions follow either cm or inch measures, but do not mix them as this may lead to small inaccuracies.

You should always check whether your sheet size corresponds to these measurements, as they are the basis of all the transparencies. If your sheet is longer, shorten it to 70 cm. This is important for the ease and accuracy of cutting out the pieces without measuring each separately. There is a broad range of colours and transparency of tissue paper which will vary depending on manufacturer. Light colours in warm and cool shades are particularly recommended.

For interesting colourful effects, read the chapter 'How to enliven the Tissue Paper' (p. 11).

You will need a scalpel, a knife with a long pointed blade, to cut up the large sheets into smaller pieces. This is also useful to help folding and smoothing down fine and sharply tapered folds. In addition, you will need a razor blade, used completely flat, to carefully and neatly cut open certain folds. Cutters or other cutting tools are not suitable.

Use a light-coloured, strong piece of cardboard as a base and place a transparent A3 (16 in × 10½ in) plastic film over it for assembling the single sheets of the transparencies.
You will also need clear-drying craft glue.

To ensure precise gluing, use a long wooden stick with a pointed end to glue the marked points and to assemble the stars. You can sharpen the end with a knife after repeated use.

One-sided, transparent adhesive tape about ½ in (12 mm) wide is particularly good for fixing the transparency to the window.

You may also need a pair of scissors to cut the triangular pieces, a ruler is only needed for checking the sizes.

To enliven of the colours of the tissue paper, you will need a medium-sized paintbrush, a small sponge and a hairdryer for speedy drying. Use watercolours in a small dish if desired, or other liquid water-soluble colours (e.g. Ecoline).

Explaining the Symbols

ø   aproximate diameter of the finished star

(C)   centre, and gluing point for sticking the star together

(P)   point of the star

O   gluing point

⊙   gluing point between the base and the first layer of paper

⊙   important orientation point and gluing point between two star-points when assembling does not follow the usual pattern

↰   the arrow shows the direction to fold

↻   fold and unfold (preparation fold for an orientation fold)

↻   turn the sheet over between two sets of folding

⇒   pull out a fold for a special light effect

▬   smooth down with the back of a knife

▭   cut a slit with a knife or scalpel

▱   press with thumb for a 'trumpet fold'

How to enliven the Tissue Paper

It is important to choose the right colours to enhance the patterns of the transparencies. Light orange, pale pink, light blue as well as light green will give a good contrast between light and shade. The darker the colours, the flatter or duller the transparencies will appear, although the outlines will remain strong. This is especially true for red, blue and purple shades, so you may want to enliven these colours.

At the start of each transparency you will find several examples with practical tips on how to enhance the individual effect of a star or a sun, a crystal or a flower.

The easiest procedure is to lighten the tissue paper sheet before cutting. To do this, place your sheet flat on a tiled floor and try out the following:

If you want a fine drop-like appearance on the tissue paper, sprinkle drops of water over the sheet with a wet paintbrush. For larger marks vigorously shake the brush. A cloudier appearance can be achieved with a small wet sponge. If you want a marbled effect, press a wet sponge down firmly but regularly to make splashes of water. Large drops of water will spread out further. Control these splashes and remove excess water with your sponge.

You can make a multi-coloured marbled effect using the same technique with two different coloured tissue papers, or a white and a coloured tissue paper, placed on top of each other and wetted together as described above. You can also place your chosen colour between two different colours and wet all three sheets from both sides.

This will produce interesting effects on the other tissue papers as well as your original sheet, which you can then use for different transparency projects.

Dry the wet paper with a hairdryer directly after wetting. Only lift up the paper once it is thoroughly dry. Do not forget to clean the tiles with water immediately, this will prevent the tissue paper from leaving coloured stains.

Another decorative enhancement can be achieved by additionally colouring the paper. To do this, dip the sponge in a small dish of watercolour and dab it on the parts of the paper you want coloured. You can also use different shades of colour on top of each other.

With all of these techniques the paper will wrinkle slightly and contract a few millimetres. After drying quickly with a hairdryer, flatten the paper with your hands as smooth as possible. The rest of the wrinkles can be carefully, but easily ironed out, with or without steam.

Once you have some practice folding with normal paper, the slight irregularities which ensue after enlivening the tissue paper will not deter you, but the finished transparencies will be slightly smaller than stated because the tissue paper shrinks after being treated in this way.

Cutting up the Tissue Paper

Once you have chosen the colour for your transparency you can start preparing the large sheets of tissue paper. First fold the whole sheet (normal size 20" × 27", 50 cm × 70 cm) in half and slit it in two (or four, if that is what you need; see basic pattern, p. 12) with a sharp knife. Make sure the edges are exactly aligned before cutting. Continue dividing the sheet according to the individual patterns.

This simple method avoids having to measure with a ruler. The sizes given are achieved automatically and are only stated in case you want to check your results.

The basic pattern and number of sheets needed are given under each individual instruction and are shown by the following symbols:

You can choose between two, sometimes four, circumferences (ø). Beginners should start with a simple transparency (* to **) and choose the middle size.

Basic Cutting Patterns

There are two sketches at the beginning of each pattern. The upper sketch refers to the large sheet of tissue paper 20" × 28" (cut to this length from 30"), or 50 cm × 70 cm. It shows the amount and size of single small sheets to be obtained from a quarter, a half or the whole of the large sheet. The lower sketch shows an enlargement of the small sheet with measurements.

As such these measurements are superfluous as they are achieved automatically by dividing the paper as shown. They are only mentioned in case you want to check your sizes.

The colour of the sketches makes it easier to see the basic shape required.

The basic pattern number used in each transparency is given at the start of each instruction behind the circumference size (ø).

Rectangular sheets

These can have different sizes and even be long thin strips of tissue paper. The basic cutting Patterns 1–8 (p. 14) give sheets that are easily obtained by dividing the paper repeatedly. For the long strips (Patterns 15 and 16), half or quarter of the large sheet is halved (red line) and then folded and cut into thirds (p. 15). Check whether the folds are evenly spaced with a ruler. Do not worry if you need to re-fold repeatedly, it will not affect the finished appearance of the transparency.

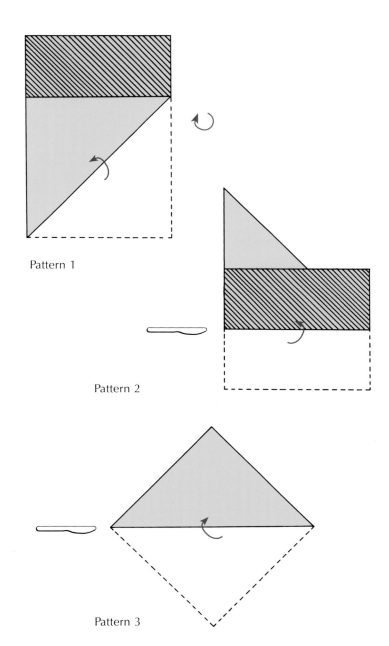

Pattern 1

Pattern 2

Square and triangular sheets

Basic Patterns 9–14 (p. 15) show how to make squares and triangles. Fold and cut, using a knife, half or a quarter of the large sheet following Patterns 1 and 2 (right). All you need to do then is continue folding the large square into four or sixteen pieces, depending on the instructions. The shaded part remains unused.

The triangles are made by folding the squares in half diagonally as shown in Pattern 3 (right). Use a pair of scissors if the ends of the diagonals prove hard to slit with a knife.

Pattern 3

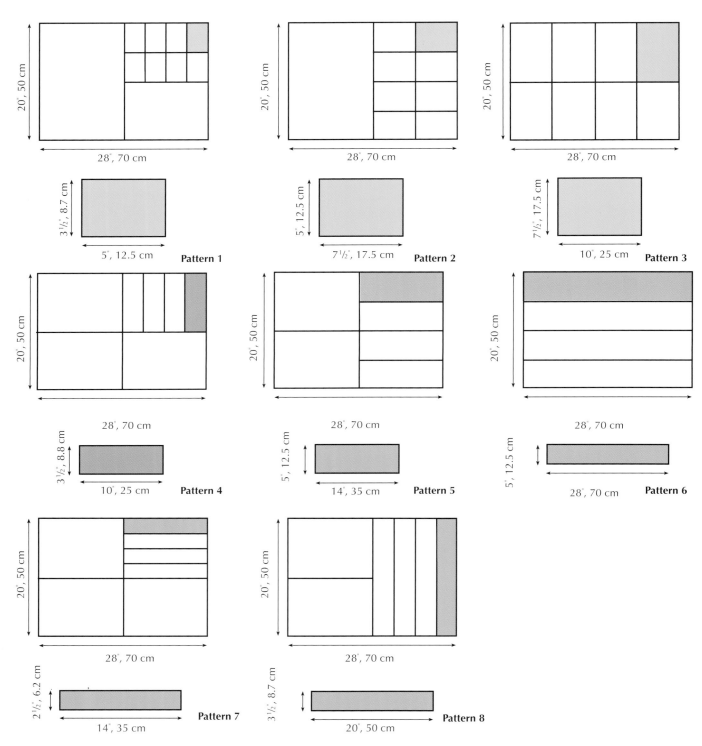

20", 50 cm
28", 70 cm
3½", 8.7 cm
5", 12.5 cm
Pattern 1

20", 50 cm
28", 70 cm
5", 12.5 cm
7½", 17.5 cm
Pattern 2

20", 50 cm
28", 70 cm
7½", 17.5 cm
10", 25 cm
Pattern 3

20", 50 cm
28", 70 cm
3½", 8.8 cm
10", 25 cm
Pattern 4

20", 50 cm
28", 70 cm
5", 12.5 cm
14", 35 cm
Pattern 5

20", 50 cm
28", 70 cm
5", 12.5 cm
28", 70 cm
Pattern 6

20", 50 cm
28", 70 cm
2½", 6.2 cm
14", 35 cm
Pattern 7

20", 50 cm
28", 70 cm
3½", 8.7 cm
20", 50 cm
Pattern 8

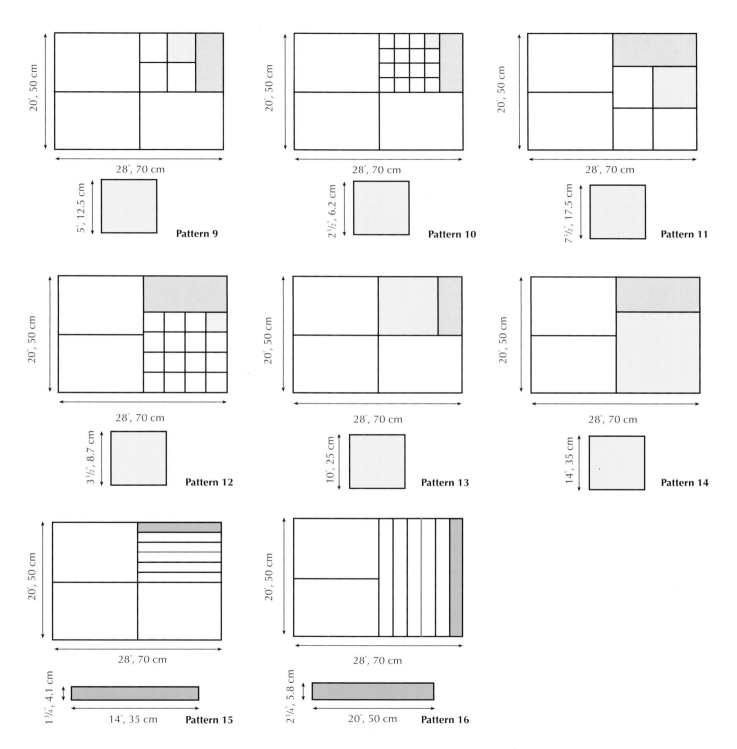

20", 50 cm
28", 70 cm
5", 12.5 cm
Pattern 9

20", 50 cm
28", 70 cm
2½", 6.2 cm
Pattern 10

20", 50 cm
28", 70 cm
7½", 17.5 cm
Pattern 11

20", 50 cm
28", 70 cm
3½", 8.7 cm
Pattern 12

20", 50 cm
28", 70 cm
10", 25 cm
Pattern 13

20", 50 cm
28", 70 cm
14", 35 cm
Pattern 14

20", 50 cm
28", 70 cm
1¾", 4.1 cm
14", 35 cm
Pattern 15

20", 50 cm
28", 70 cm
2¼", 5.8 cm
20", 50 cm
Pattern 16

15

Assembling the Sheets

Once all the sheets have been folded the exciting moment has come to assemble the whole transparency. Put the plastic film on the cardboard before starting to assemble. Place the folded side of the sheets up, then glue them together clockwise.

Transparencies with eight points

Place the first sheet flat in front of you, with the centre (C) facing. With the help of the wooden stick, dab two small dots of glue on the underside of the second sheet, exactly at the centre (C) and the corner (Figure 1).

1.

Now stick the two sheets together so that the centre points are exactly on top of each other. At the same time, the left edge of the second sheet should be exactly above the centre fold-line of the first sheet. Proceed in the same way for the other sheets (Figure 2).

2.

16

When gluing the eighth and last sheet, place the left edge of the very first sheet on top. To so this, lift this first sheet up a bit and push the last sheet under it (Figure 3).

3.

Carefully turn the transparency over. Stick the edges of the points together with a few dots or strips of glue (Figure 4).

Before you can fully admire your transparency, read the chapter 'Fixing the Transparency to the Window.' (p.19)

Transparencies with sixteen points

Stick the sheets together in the same way as the eight-pointed transparencies, the gluing points are again on the centre fold-line of the previous sheets. Be careful not to glue the sixteen sheets too close together.

4.

Transparencies with five and six points

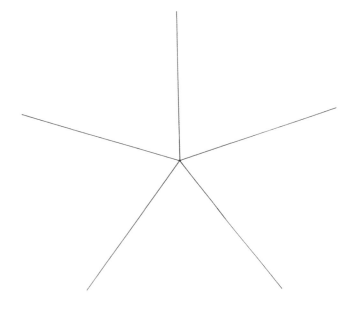

The principle of assembling remains the same. But as you will not be able to use the centre fold-line as an orientation line you will need to use a diagram. Enlarge the five- and six-pointed diagrams left and above with a photocopier. Lengthen the lines with a red pen and place the diagram you need under the plastic film. Now place the centre fold-lines exactly on these red lines to obtain a five-pointed star or a snowflake.

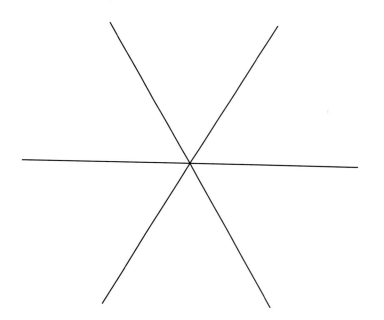

Transparencies with three, four and eleven points

The centre fold-lines are again of no help for assembling these stars. But the step-by-step instructions of each individual star include a figure showing the orientation points (or lines) for sticking together. These orientation and gluing points are the hidden key for assembling the transparency successfully.

Fixing the Transparency to the Window

The elusive appearance of the tissue paper transparency only reveals itself properly when hanging in the window with daylight streaming through it. The details shine through best when the flat side is stuck to the windowpane. Three-dimensional transparencies can only be hung this way round, leaving the loose folds on the front.

Stick short strips of adhesive tape to every second or third point, at a place where the tissue paper is not too thin. Now roll short pieces of adhesive tape together to make two-sided sticky patches. Place these onto the adhesive tape strips. These patches can be re-used. You can change the position of your transparency without problem and protect the fine paper of your transparency. This way the transparencies will withstand repeated use for years.

The colours will fade after some months. But this 'autumnal process' also has its attractions. Some unexpected folded nuances can suddenly appear beautifully.

The transparencies look different depending on the light conditions: from early morning sun to dusk new impressions are conjured up. Even light from a street lamp can turn the transparency into a mysterious presence in your window.

1. Rays of strength *

EIGHT-POINTED

ø 20¹⁄₂", 51 cm, Pattern 3
ø 14¹⁄₂", 36 cm, Pattern 2
ø 10¹⁄₂", 26 cm, Pattern 1

The transparency's appeal lies in the clear and unusual structure of its eight points, which looks like a sudden spark lighting up the darkness! The radial shape is reminiscent of a trumpet's clear, triumphant, angelic sound.

Use light-coloured tissue paper for this transparency. You can make beautiful colour combinations by placing two matching coloured sheets of transparency paper on top of each other (e.g. light green and light blue), and wetting both liberally with a sponge (see p. 11 for instructions).

You will need eight rectangular pieces of tissue paper, following Pattern 1, 2 or 3 depending on the desired circumference of the star. Size 1 is the best for a beginner.

Fold each sheet in half lengthways and unfold again. Centre and diagonal folds are always important orientation lines to start with before the actual folding process begins. At the start of each instruction for making transparencies you will find a small sketch, showing whether to start with a centre or a diagonal fold-line.

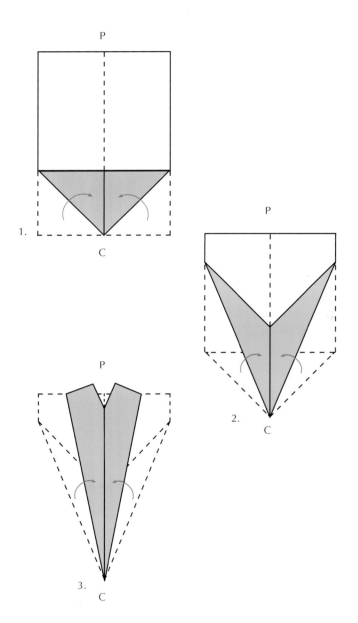

1-3. Fold the star following the step-by-step folding instructions shown by the figures. The dotted lines indicate the previous fold. Coloured parts and arrows clarify the folding process.

4. Lift up the right side and fold out the hidden corner to the left. This folding out process is always shown by the symbol ⇛.

5. Fold this left corner back over to the right side. *Similarly fold out the left side, and fold it back to the left.*

6. Fold the centre edges to the sides. Use the back of a knife to help make crisply tapered folds. Fold the diagonal edges at the centre (C) to the two dotted fold-lines. Now glue the marked points (O).

7. Once you have finished folding the eight sheets, you can start assembling. Basic instructions are given on p. 16. The last figure always shows two assembled sheets. The second sheet (P2) is indicted by a blue dotted line.

Make sure the red dotted fold-lines are placed exactly on top of each other. Apply glue sparingly to the three marked points.

You can now admire your first star in the window.

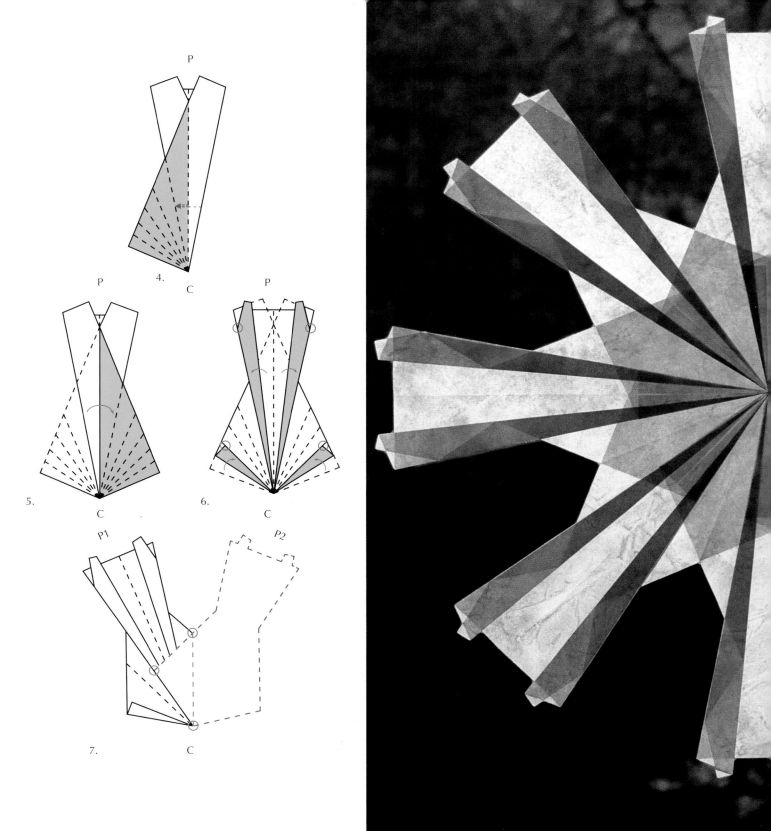

P

4.

C

P

5.

C

P

6.

C

P1

P2

7.

C

2. Sunshine * *

SIXTEEN-POINTED

ø 20", 50 cm, Pattern 3
ø 14", 35 cm, Pattern 2
ø 10", 25 cm, Pattern 1

This sunny transparency strongly contrasts with the previous transparency 'rays of strength.' The sharp dynamics of the former have been transformed into a harmonious and peaceful shining.

Bright yellow tissue paper suits this dazzling transparency. But if you prefer a marbled effect, place a darker yellow sheet onto a lemon yellow sheet and wet them both (see p. 11). The large sun (ø 20", 50 cm) is particularly beautiful if the tissue paper is coloured strongly. For example, I used a white and a dark orange sheet of tissue paper wetted together, with an unexpected but spectacular result (photo p. 24).

Cut sixteen rectangular sheets following the patterns above. Fold each sheet in half to obtain a guiding centre fold and continue folding following the detailed step-by-step instructions on the next page.

1. Preparation folds.

2–3. Fold as shown.

4. Fold over the four corners and glue the marked points.

5. Preparation fold for folding the centre (C).

6. Fold the two side corners to the newly made fold-lines. Make sure the edges of these folds meet the corners of the (P) folds exactly without overlapping. Glue.

7. Fold over both (C) flaps and glue the three marked points.

8. Fold the point (P) down to the part where the two (C) flaps meet in the centre and unfold.

9. Fold as shown.

10. Gluing the sixteen points together is simple and follows the usual pattern.

— Tip:

Because of the amount of sheets, do not glue them too closely together. The edge and centre fold-line should be kept slightly apart to avoid irregularities at the centre of this sun.

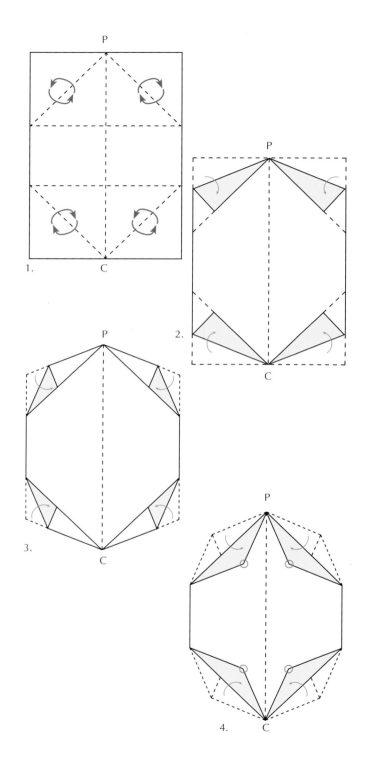

26

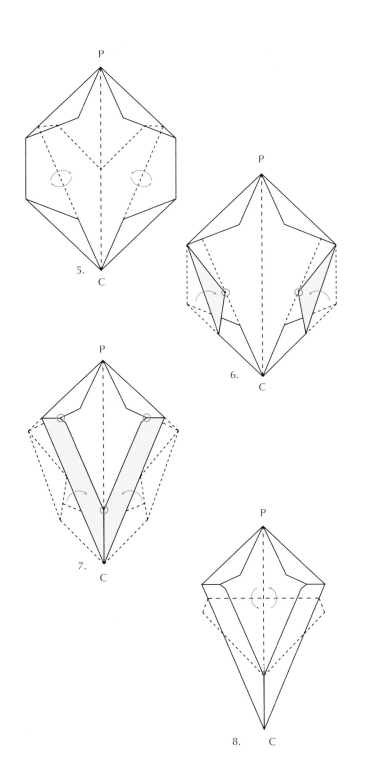

5.

6.

7.

8.

9.

10.

3. Still peace *

EIGHT-POINTED

ø 20", 50 cm, Pattern 3
ø 14", 35 cm, Pattern 2
ø 10", 25 cm, Pattern 1

The points of this star play around a slightly emphasized central circle, which makes the transparency look like a peacefully held wheel. There is also a delightful polarity between the inside and the outside of the star.

Choose a light coloured tissue paper to allow the structure of the central circle to be clearly seen.

Cut eight sheets following the pattern above and fold the centre fold-lines.

1–2. Preparation folds. Unfold again completely.

3. Fold both (P) corners to the second fold-line, as shown.

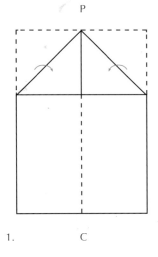

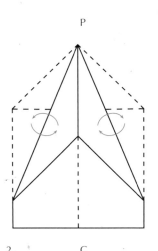

29

4. Continue folding as shown, using the back of a knife to stop the previous fold from slipping.

5–6. Continue folding the point (P) as shown. Then glue the single marked point.

7–8–9. Now fold the centre (C). Finish by gluing the four marked points.

10. This star is very simple to assemble (see basic instructions, p. 16).

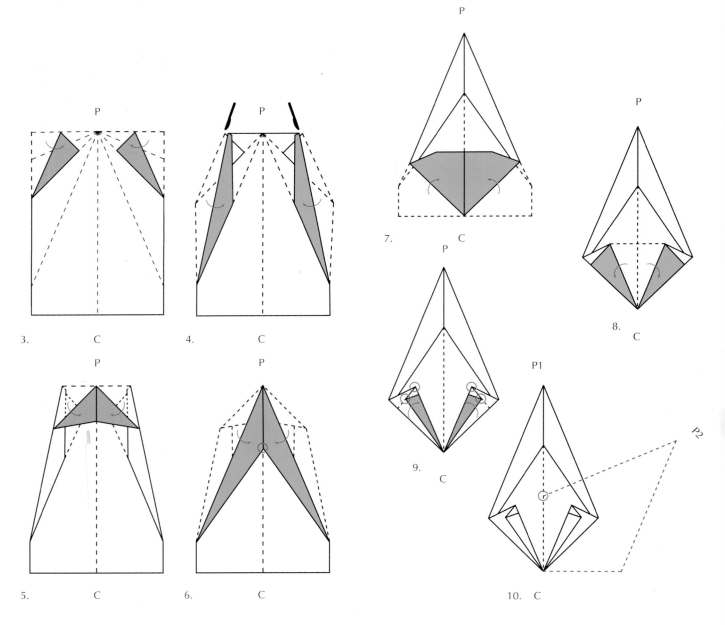

4. Daisy * * * *

ELEVEN-POINTED

ø 14", 35 cm, Pattern 2
ø 10", 25 cm, Pattern 1

The folding process of the previous star 'peaceful stillness' is continued and transformed to make this flower-like transparency. The star-points are now closer to nature and have become a shining daisy. The beautiful heart of the flower can be made even more effective by slightly opening the central folds for a three-dimensional appearance.

Always use white tissue paper for this transparency. You will need eleven small sheets of tissue paper, which is two quarter pieces of the large tissue paper sheet for the daisy (smaller size), and two half pieces of the large sheets for the marguerite (larger size). Fold the large sheet into the sections for the smaller sheets and then colour with watercolours before cutting.

The figures on the right show the width of the strips in the large sheet to dab with colour.

Colours for the daisy (Pattern 1, top): dark yellow (Ecoline 202), for the points of the petals: pastel pink (Ecoline 390)

For the marguerite (Pattern 2, below): yellow (Ecoline 259), then add a hint of orange (Ecoline 236).

Always dry the sheets immediately with a hair dryer, this prevents unsightly marks on the pure white tissue paper. Carefully iron the sheets to avoid unwanted creases. Now slit the sheet with a knife and choose eleven of the nicest coloured pieces.

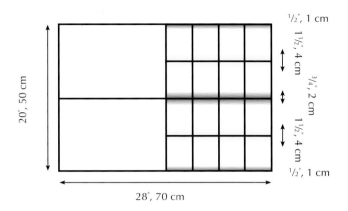

Pattern 1. Daisy

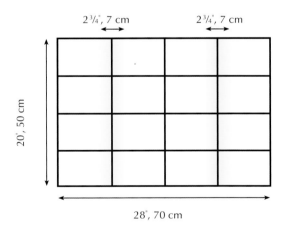

Pattern 2. Marguerite

0. Start with the first fold of 'still peace' (p. 29)

1. Fold back the two flaps (see next page).

2. Preparation fold. Fold the point (P) down to the inner meeting point of the corners. Unfold. You now have a short orientation fold.

3. Reposition the inner meeting point of the corners to the new meeting point at the orientation fold. (See arrows).

4. Fold as shown.

5. Preparation folds for the sides.

6. Fold the diagonal edges to the newly made folds. Use the back of a knife to help you make a crisp fold.

7. Open up the point (P) by carefully pulling out the two top flaps and folding down their upper corners at the horizontal top (P) as neatly as possible. There will be a slight overlap at the lower side corners. Now start folding the centre (C) as shown.

8–9. Fold as shown.

10. Move both centre (C) flaps until their inner edges are on the centre fold. Glue the marked point without gluing the loose flaps.

11. Preparation fold. Fold the right outer edge to the short diagonal edge (marked in red). Unfold. You now have a long diagonal fold-line.

12. Make a 'trumpet fold.' Lift up the right edge with your forefinger to above the diagonal fold-line made previously and press it down exactly onto this line. During the transition phase of this folding process a trumpet shape appears, which disappears again once the fold is flattened.

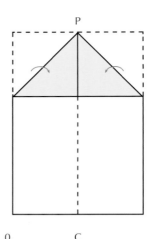

0.

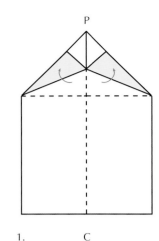

1.

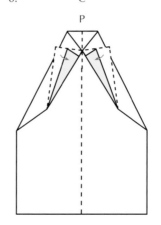

4.

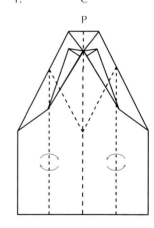

5.

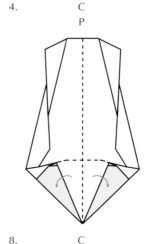

8.

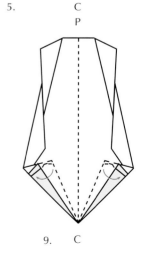

9.

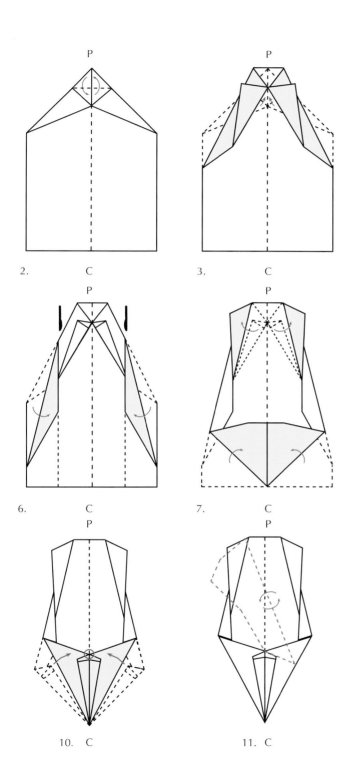

2.   C

3.   C

6.   C

7.   C

10.   C

11.   C

12.   C

The figure shows the right side only. *Repeat the folding process of Figures 11 and 12 again on the left side.* To finish, glue the four marked points.

13. Assembling the transparency. Because of the uneven number of sheets in this transparency you will need to locate specific orientation points to assemble.

You will find the first orientation point for Pattern 1 (daisy) on the right diagonal edge, $^1/_4$" (7 mm) away from the centre fold-line. Mark this point lightly with a pencil (shown in red in the figure).

The orientation point for Pattern 2 (marguerite) is on the same diagonal line $^3/_8$" (1 cm) away from the centre fold-line.

Glue all eleven sheets together in this way. Lift up the loose centre flaps with your forefinger whilst gluing to avoid gluing them too.

Turn the transparency over and strengthen it with long strips of glue.

Once the 'daisy' or 'marguerite' is stuck to the window, pull out and sort the loose yellow-orange folds in the centre to make an even circle. A harmonious tissue paper flower will shine back at you.

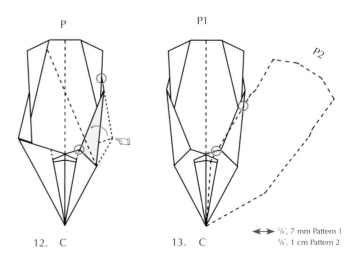

13.   C

$^1/_4$", 7 mm Pattern 1
$^3/_8$", 1 cm Pattern 2

35

5. Crystal chimes * *

SIX-POINTED

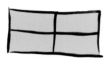

ø 13 ³/₄", 34.5 cm, Pattern 3
ø 9 ³/₄", 24.5 cm, Pattern 2
ø 7", 17.5 cm, Pattern 1

This extraordinary six-pointed star awakens a musical winter feeling in the observer because of its rigid, finely cut structure. Which distant magic sounds are created by the crystal's crisp coolness? And in its midst a gentle flower shimmers, budding and yet still hidden ...

A light, cold-coloured tissue paper will allow this crystal transparency to show off its clear form. You can also experiment with different colour nuances by placing white tissue paper onto light blue, or light blue onto pale pink and thoroughly but unsystematically wetting both sheets (see instructions, p. 11). This method produces fascinating colour combinations that enhance the mysterious attraction of the transparency.

First fold two centre fold-lines into the six sheets.

1. Fold as shown and glue.

2–3. Continue folding at the point (P). Use the back of a knife for help.

4. The last fine fold of the point (P). Now start folding the centre (C).

5. Preparation folds.

6. Fold in the edges to the newly made fold-line. Glue.

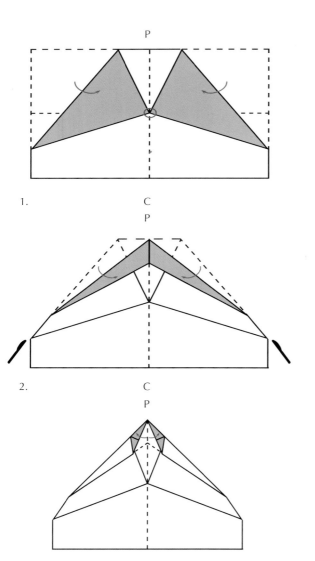

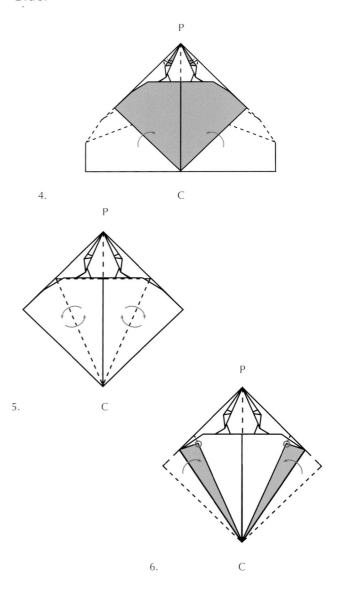

7. Fold out the two flaps as shown.

8–9. Continue folding as shown. To finish, glue the marked corners as shown.

To assemble, use the diagram for a six-pointed star (see basic instructions, p. 18)

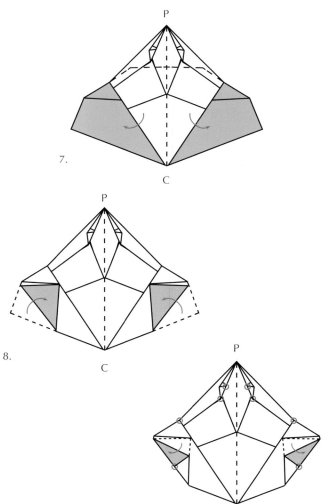

6. Clover leaf * * *

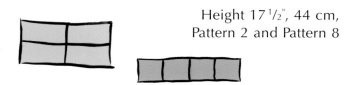

Height 17 ½", 44 cm,
Pattern 2 and Pattern 8

The clover leaf will look fresh and lively in your window. This piece of spring green folding artwork transports you into the refreshing atmosphere of a wide meadow.

These three transparency sheets are a simplified form of the previous transparency 'crystal chimes.' Use light green tissue paper, or squeeze a wet sponge over a juicy green-coloured tissue paper for a beautiful effect (see instructions, p. 11).

➤ *Folding the three clover leaves:*

Start by folding the two centre folds in the tissue paper sheets of Pattern 2, and then follow Figure 1 of 'crystal chimes' (p. 38). Remember to glue the marked point!

1. Fold as shown.

2–3. Preparation folds.

4. Glue the two small corners to the fold-line.

5. Fold out the flaps as shown.

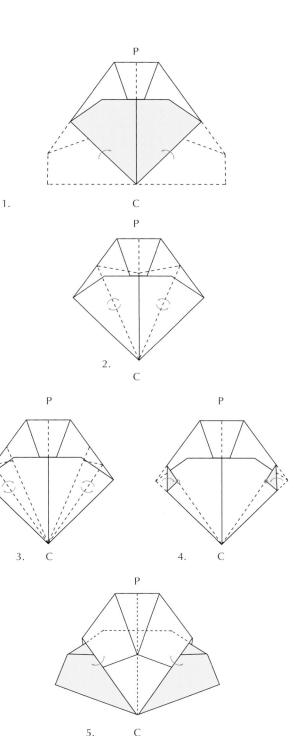

6. Fold the two corners up to the point where the side edges meet the folds below (shines through). Glue.

After this and on the right side only fold the preparation fold for gluing the sheets together as shown by the blue dotted line. To do this, fold the right (C) edge up to the inner edge and unfold. To finish, glue all the loose folds on the reverse side of the sheets with strips of glue.

— *Folding the stalk:*

You will need half of Pattern 8 for the stalk, so slit it lengthways with a sharp knife. Then fold the three vertical folds as shown by the above sketch.

7. Start with the right side of the strip. Fold the upper edge down until it reaches the end of the centre fold (red arrow). At the same time ensure the fold is done carefully at the corners to make a perfectly tapered diagonal. You will probably need several attempts before the fold is correct. Do not worry about this as the tissue paper is extremely flexible.

8–9–10. Fold as shown, taking care to be precise. Use the back of a knife if necessary.

11. Fold the right side up until its lower edge makes a straight line with the rest of the sheet. Glue. If there is a tiny corner sticking out at the very point (this point is marked with an arrow) cut it off with a pair of scissors.

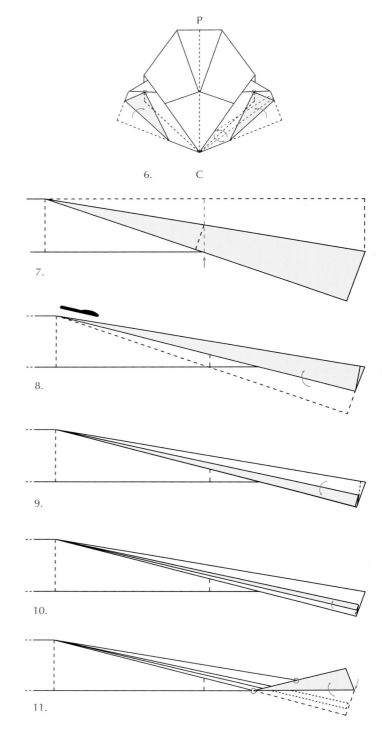

Repeat the folding process of Figures 7 to 11 on the left side.

12. *Right side only.* To finish, lift the right side up to the vertical fold-line and stick it with a strip of glue. The stalk is finished.

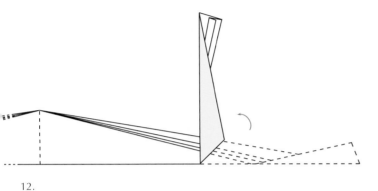

12.

— *Assembling:*

13. Glue the three leaves together, using the right orientation line as a guide (see blue dotted line, Figure 6). If you have used water *on* the tissue paper before cutting out the individual sheets, then there will be a tiny gap about $^1/_{16}$" (2 mm) wide between the edge of the leaf and the orientation line. Place your hand onto the leaves to ensure they remain as flat as possible. Do not use too much glue at the centre.

Stick the stalk to the leaves by placing its right end on the upper right diagonal fold of one of the leaves and the centre part *behind* the next leaf, as the figure clearly shows.

The clover leaf in the window gives a welcoming 'green greeting!'

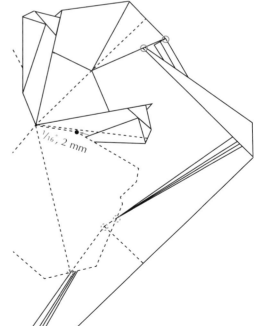

13.

7. Frost flower * *

SIX-POINTED

ø 12 ¹/₂", 31.5 cm, Pattern 3
ø 9 ³/₄", 24.5 cm, Pattern 2
ø 7", 17.5 cm, Pattern 1

The night frost has painted icy figures onto the window pane. This transparency is the clearest remaining snowy crystal, whose powerful points radiate inwards and hold a delicate star imprisoned in their midst.

This transparency is an interesting variation on the two previous transparencies. The unfolded points leave enough space to beautifully marble the background, which you can do by de-colouring the tissue paper with a wet sponge before cutting the sheets. Or you can make a delicate colour combination by placing a light blue tissue paper between two pink tissue papers and wetting them all well with a sponge (see instructions, p. 11).

Cut six rectangular sheets, following Pattern 1, 2 or 3. First fold both centre fold-lines and then follow Figures 1 and 2 of 'crystal chimes' (p. 38). *However, here the point (P) and the centre (C) are reversed.*

1. Fold as shown. Glue at the centre.

2. Preparation folds. *Now turn the sheet over.*

3. Fold the side flaps to the newly made fold-lines and glue. *Now turn the sheet back over.*

4. Fold back the flaps at the point (P).

5. Fold the side corners inwards.

6. Fold back the side edges as shown. Glue the four marked points.
   Assemble the star using the diagram for a six-pointed star (see basic pattern, p. 18)

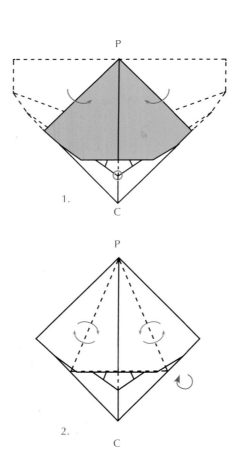

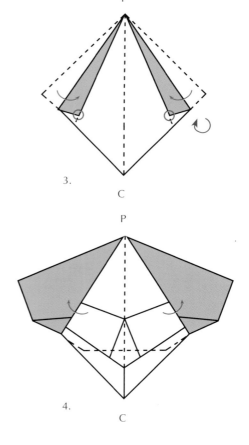

46

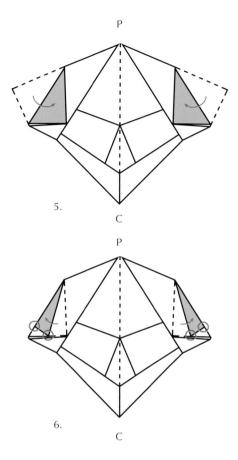

5.

6.

8. Morning star * *

FIVE-POINTED

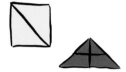

ø 19", 48 cm, Pattern 11
ø 14", 35 cm, Pattern 9
ø 10", 25 cm, Pattern 12
ø 6¹/₂", 16 cm, Pattern 10

This graceful star with its shimmering appearance is like the first beautiful rays of the morning star above the early morning horizon.

Despite the amount of points this is not a complicated star to fold. First make a base with five sheets, and then add the five larger points. Because of the two-tiered make-up, it is possible to make a two-coloured star. It is best to choose two light colours that suit together. But you can also make a single coloured star, for example, from carmine red tissue paper, which is heavily wetted before cutting out the sheets. Another beautiful colour combination can be achieved by wetting two large sheets of tissue paper together, e.g. pink and mauve-blue to make a blue-purple star (see instructions, p. 11).

You will need five square sheets for the points, as shown above. For the base make three of the same sized square sheets and halve them to obtain triangles (see instructions, p. 13).

⌐ Folding the base:

0. Take five triangles and fold the two preparation folds. Unfold.

1. Fold the (P) edges to the centre fold-line. *Now turn the sheet over.*

2. Fold as shown. Glue. *Turn the sheet back over.*

3. Fold back both flaps as far as possible. Glue the two concealed marked points.
   You can finish the base now by gluing the folded sheets together using the diagram for a five-pointed star (see basic instructions, p. 18). Do not use too much glue in the centre.

⌐ Folding the points of the star:

Make five square sheets and fold a single diagonal fold-line on each of them.

4. Fold as shown. *Turn the sheet over.*

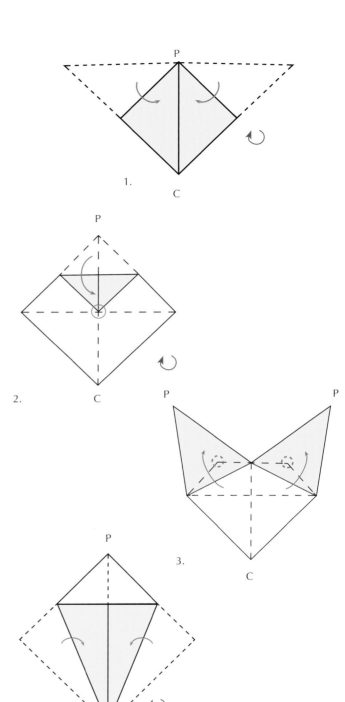

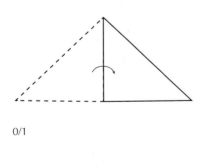

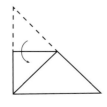

5–6. Fold the point (P) on the reverse side. After gluing the marked points *turn the sheet back over.*

7. Fold out both flaps as shown. Glue.

— *Assembling:*

8. Place the centre (C) of each point onto the centre of the base, with the centre fold-lines exactly on top of each other. Turn the transparency over to glue the concealed marked point on the reverse side.

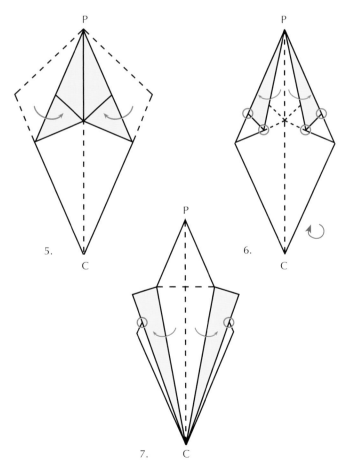

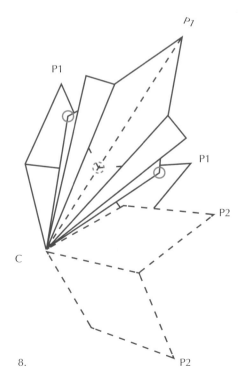

9. Three kings' star * * *

FIVE-POINTED

Star ø 10", 25 cm, Pattern 12, plus tail length 18¹/₂", 46 cm, Pattern 14

Star ø 6¹/₂", 16 cm, Pattern 10, plus tail length 13¹/₂", 34 cm, Pattern 13

A comet travels through the night, leading the way with its shining tail.

This transparency is the previous star made with yellow-orange tissue paper with a large triangular sheet attached to make the comet's tail. Only two sizes are suitable for this star (Pattern 10 or 12), unlike the four given for the previous star.

For the tail, take a square sheet (Pattern 13 or 14), and halve it diagonally to obtain a triangle (see instructions, p. 13)

Follow the detailed figures. Use the back of a knife to fold the sharply tapered folds.

0. Start with three preparation folds. Unfold all the folds again. You now have seven orientation folds.

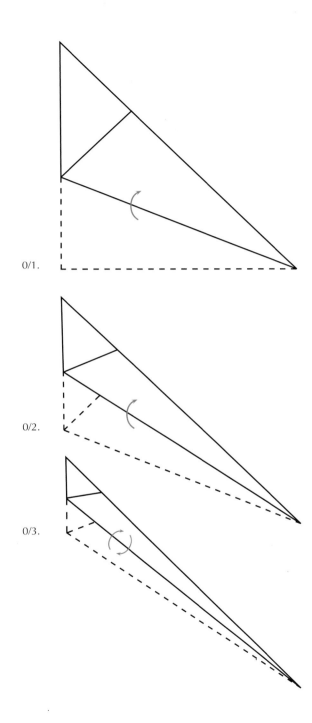

0/1.

0/2.

0/3.

1. Fold the outer edges as shown.

2. Fold the upper fold back to the outer edge. Fold the second orientation fold onto the third orientation fold. Now fold the fifth fold-line downwards onto the fourth fold-line. Glue all marked points. You can strengthen the folds with a strip of glue along the entire length.

4–7. Four preparation folds to enable the correct centre fold at (C). Make these orientation folds crisp and clear.

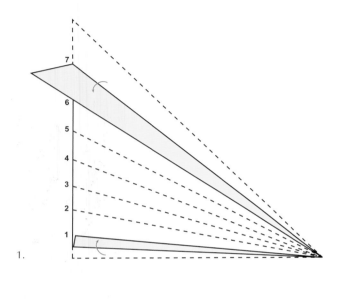

1.

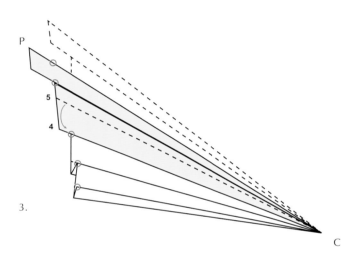

3.

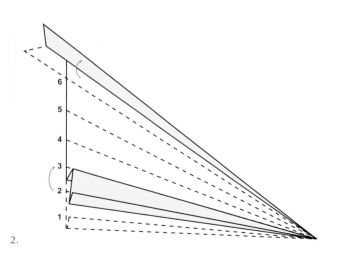

2.

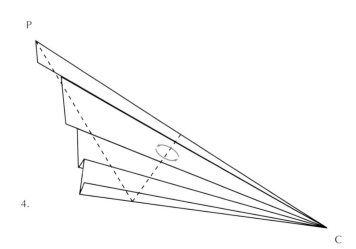

4.

P

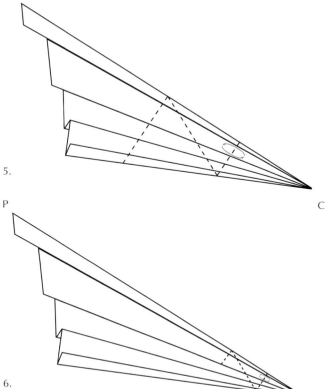

5.

P

6.

C

P

7.

C

8. Last fold. Stick with a dot and a strip of glue.

9. Glue the tail *behind* one of the long rays at the left edge, as the figure clearly shows.

P

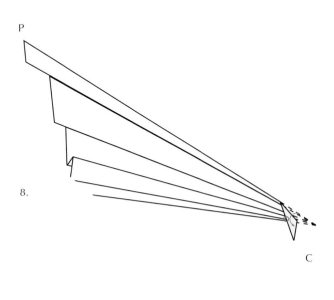

8.

C

P

P

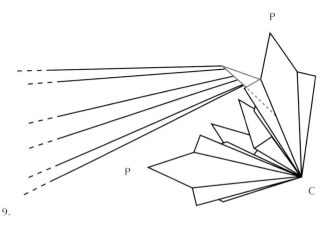

9.

C

10. Dahlia rosette * * *

ELEVEN-POINTED

ø 15 1/2", 39 cm, Pattern 5
ø 11", 27.5 cm, Pattern 4

How the sun's rays wove the heart of this rosette remains a secret. But with the tissue paper rustling between your fingers sheet by sheet it is slowly created until this magnificent garden piece can bloom in your window.

Use light-coloured tissue paper for this double folded transparency. For a more interesting colour, dab drops of similar coloured watercolour over the tissue paper, or de-colour the paper with drops of water (see instructions, p. 11).

Cut eleven rectangular pieces following Pattern 4 or 5. Fold in half lengthways for the centre fold-line. Unfold and then fold twice widthways for three vertical fold-lines. Make sure these folds are very crisp. Unfold.

1. Fold the two horizontal preparation folds.

2. Fold the outer edges to the first orientation folds as shown.

3. First fold back the four small corners and glue the marked points. Then make the four preparation folds from the corners to the centre fold-line as shown. Unfold.

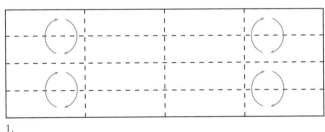

1.

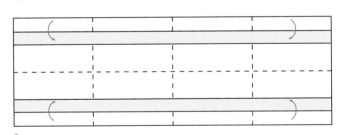

2.

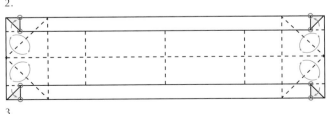

3.

4. Fold the outer edges to the newly made orientation folds. Glue.

5. Make two preparation folds by folding both outer points inwards to the meeting point between the horizontal centre fold and the vertical fold. Unfold.

6. Fold the corners to the meeting point of the newly made fold and the centre fold-line. Glue.

7. Now fold one side of the sheet over to the other side, the point should meet the meeting point of the flaps on the opposite side as shown. Glue.

8. Fold the lower edge as shown. This is now the centre (C).

9–10. Continue folding the centre (C) and glue the marked points. Because the tissue paper is thick with folds here it is best to use the blade of a knife to make the last folds exact and smooth.

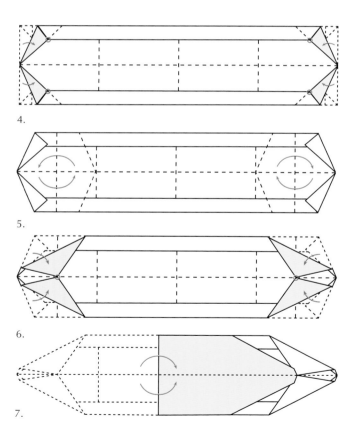

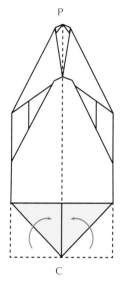

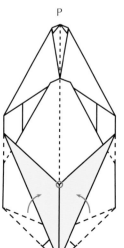

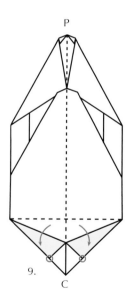

← Assembling:

11. If you did not wet the tissue paper the assembly point will be exactly on the inside diagonal edge of the first piece. If using Pattern 5 it will be about $1/16$" (2 mm) away.

If you treated the tissue paper with water before cutting out the individual sheets, your finished pieces will probably be slightly smaller. In this case push the corner of the second sheet slightly to the inside of the diagonal edge of the first sheet, about $1/16$" (2 mm) for Pattern 4 and about $1/8$" (4 mm) for Pattern 5.

It is best to glue the sheets together very lightly so that you can still adjust them all if necessary. Only once you have accurately pieced together all eleven sheets strengthen the transparency with strips of glue.

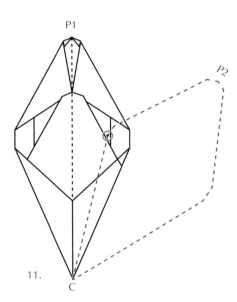

11. Carnival bow tie * * * * *

Length 13 ³/₄", 34.5 cm, Pattern 6
Length 9 ³/₄", 24.5 cm, Pattern 8
Length 7", 17.5 cm, Pattern 7

This interesting structure was the surprising result of two artistic folds created while folding for fun. This produces an amusing tissue paper bow, or maybe a pair of butterfly wings!

Any colour is suitable for this transparency as long as light can still shine through the central knot. You can experiment with the basic colour, either by de-colouring the tissue paper with water, or by painting with watercolours (see instructions, p. 11). This transparency is suitable for making into a slightly three-dimensional structure, which softens the outlines, as there are hardly any gluing points.

Take a single rectangular sheet, as shown above. The smallest size (Pattern 7) requires more skill than the other sizes because of small folds.

Fold both centre fold-lines.

1. Fold the two outer edges to the centre fold-lines.

2–3. Make very crisp preparation folds at the left-hand corners as shown. Unfold all the folds.

4. This is the first artistic fold, similar to a 'trumpet fold,' to make an arrow shape. Push your finger between the two layers of tissue paper at the left upper corner as shown and move the first layer towards the inside with the help of your finger so that the left outer edge ends up lying flat against the centre fold-line. The other edges will automatically be in the right place.

5–6. Fold back the inner edge twice. *Now repeat Figures 4–6 in the other three unfolded corners.* There are no gluing points during this procedure. Make sure the fold-lines remain exactly on top of each other, and that the layers of tissue paper do not slip apart.

7. This is how the sheet looks at this point. Now fold the four orientation folds in the centre. To do this, fold the inner edges to the long centre fold-line and unfold. *Turn the sheet over!*

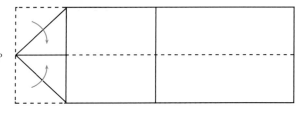

2.

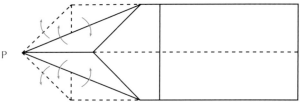

3.

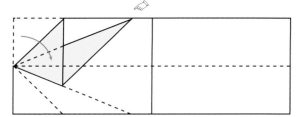

4.

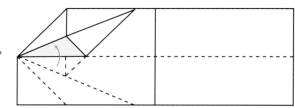

5.

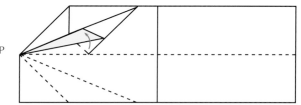

6.

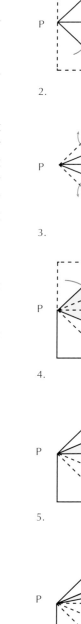

1.

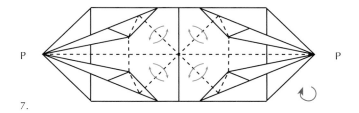

7.

Turn the finished sheet back over. Once the carnival bow tie is stuck to the window you can pull it out slightly to make it more three-dimensional.

8. To get this shape, you will need to place the newly turned sheet half onto the table in front of you so that you can pull the loose lower point out to the front. Fold this point (P) to the meeting point of the central fold-lines. Repeat this process on the other side of the sheet. Glue both points to the centre point. The sheet now has two new outer points (P).

Fold the four small corners at the new points (P) as shown on the left. Then continue folding these corners as shown on the right of the figure.

Turn the sheet back over!

9. The next folding process is divided into two steps. First fold the preparation folds for the four corners as shown on the left of the figure. Unfold.

Now make four so-called 'trumpet folds' (the second artistic fold) as shown on the right of the figure. To do this, lift up the outer edges and then press them down exactly above the preparation fold-lines below. In the transition phase you will see a 'trumpet' shape.

10. Now you will need to perfect these trumpet folds for the desired effect. Move the inner edges of each trumpet fold further inwards (direction of arrow) until the outer edges reach the small centre fold-line. Hold this edge tight with your fingers and let the trumpet fold slip back to its initial position. The four centre points should be exactly above the fold-lines below. Glue the two marked points. Fix two strips of adhesive tape to these two points.

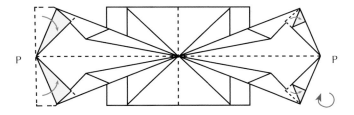

8.

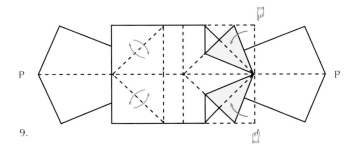

9.

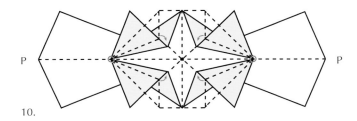

10.

12. Cross medallion * * * * *

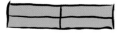

ø 13 3/4", 34.5 cm, Pattern 6
ø 9 3/4", 24.5 cm, Pattern 8
ø 6 3/4", 17 cm, Pattern 7

Noble and dainty, this balanced cross reveals a beautiful luminous quality with its clear lines in the slightly three-dimensional eight-pointed medallion.

If you have already made the previous transparency 'carnival bow tie' you will not find this transparency difficult, as it is essentially a continuation of the former.

A light-coloured tissue paper will let the central rhombus shine through particularly well. As well as the varied methods of colouring and de-colouring the tissue paper to enliven it (see p. 11), you can also try a different technique for this transparency. Take a large white sheet of tissue paper and with a sponge dab a wide strip of yellow or orange watercolour through the centre of the paper, letting the colour fade out towards the edges. The cross will appear to glow from the centre outwards.

Cut two sheets, following the patterns above. Make both centre folds and then follow Figures 1–6 of the 'carnival bow tie' (p. 62)

1. Continue folding the four inner corners as shown on the left of the figure. Then fold the two centre flaps as shown on the right of the figure. *Turn the sheet over!*

Now pull out the two points (P) as shown in Figure 8 of the previous transparency (p. 63).

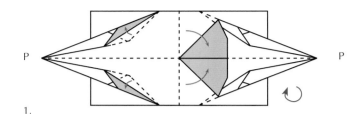

1.

2. Fold the newly created outer points (P) in two steps: first fold back the four corners as shown on the left of the figure; then continue as shown on the right.

Glue the inner points at the centre, *but only on the first sheet.* Leave them open on the second sheet for the time being. *Turn the sheet over!*

Follow Figures 9 and 10 of the previous transparency for the two next steps (p. 63).
Turn back both sheets back over!

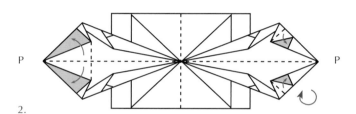

2.

3. Carefully slit the four double edges with a razor blade or sharp knife up to the meeting point with the edge of the points (P), as shown on the left of the figure (red arrow). Now make two folds on these opened corners: first as shown on the left of the figure, then the finer folds as shown on the right. Use the back of the knife to make the folds sharp and accurate.

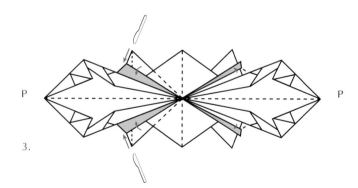

3.

4. Assembling the two finished sheets is simple. Place the sheet with the glued centre into the other sheet, lifting up the loose flaps. Place both sheets exactly centre to centre. Glue. Glue the loose points at the back to the centre. The cross medallion can be given an airier appearance by loosening the folds of the middle section into a three-dimensional structure.

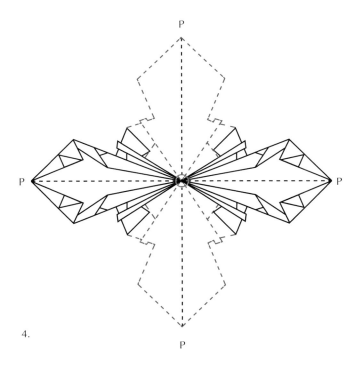

4.

Star 1 ▲   Star 3 ▼   Star 2 ▲   Star 4▼

13. Five-pointed star metamorphosis *

Star 1&2	Star 3	Star 4
ø 12", 30 cm	ø 14", 35 cm	ø 17", 42.5 cm, Pattern 11
ø 8¾", 22 cm	ø 10¼", 25.5 cm	ø 12¼", 30.5 cm, Pattern 9
ø 6", 15 cm	ø 7", 17 cm	ø 9½", 23.5 cm, Pattern 12

These four graceful flower-stars are closely related to one another, and yet each one clearly shows its own character. They are quick and easy to make and give a light and cheery impression.

There are no limits to the colour or your creativity with the tissue paper for these stars.

Depending on star size, make five square sheets of tissue paper following the pattern of your choice above and make two diagonal fold-lines on each of them.

▬ *Folding star 1*

1–2. Fold as shown and glue.

3. Preparation folds: fold the outer edges to the diagonal fold-line. Unfold.

4. Fold the edges to the orientation folds. Use the tip of a knife if needed. Glue. Assemble the star (see assembling section at the end of these instructions).

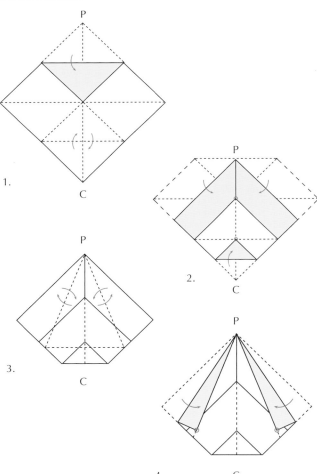

➤ Folding star 2

This star is a continuation of the previous star. Start by following Figures 1–4.

5. Now make the preparation fold lines for the centre (C).

6. Continue as shown for the centre (C) and point (P). Glue the four marked points, finished!

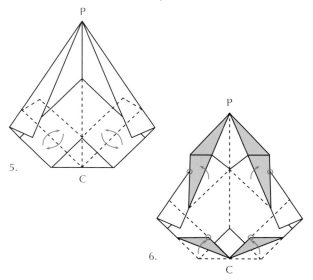

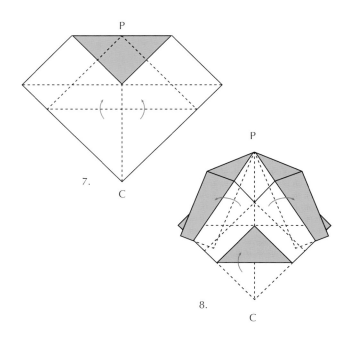

9. Lift up the inner point as shown (⟹) to fold out the edge folds. Flatten the upper (P) fold with your finger to bend the new point (P) up and back.
   Finish folding the centre (C). Glue the five marked points. You will need to turn the sheet over to glue the concealed point at (P), which makes the subtle tiny triangle visible.

➤ Folding star 3

Fold two diagonal fold-lines on all five square sheets.

7. First fold the point (P). Preparation fold for the centre (C). *Now follow the Figures 1–4 of star 1 for the point (P) only (p. 69).*

8. Fold out the inner edges of the point (P). Fold the centre (C) to the lower meeting point of the fold-lines.

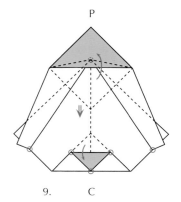

Folding star 4

Fold both diagonal fold-lines. Follow Figure 1 of star 1 (p. 69). Make the preparation fold line for the centre (C) as shown and fold the two side edges as shown for the point (P) in star 1.

10. Continue folding as shown.

11. Make two preparation folds: First fold the right upper edge to the meeting point of the diagonal fold-lines, then unfold. *Repeat this process on the left side.*

12. Fold and glue the side edges to the newly made orientation folds.

Assembling:

Use the five-pointed diagram to glue these four stars together (see basic patterns, p. 18).

You will see that the orientation point of the centre (C) is either a point (stars 2 and 3) or the diagonal fold-line (stars 1 and 4).

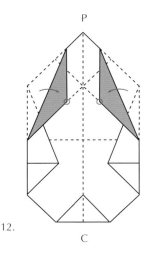

12.

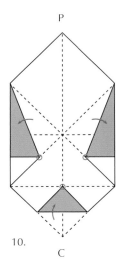

10.

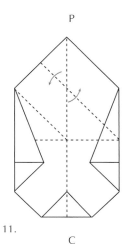

11.

14. Engraved star * * *

SIX-POINTED

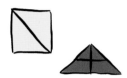

ø 17 3/4", 44.5 cm, Pattern 9
ø 12 1/2", 31.5 cm, Pattern 12

This finely structured star has a radiating appearance. Its presence in the window can also give the impression of airiness, as if the star were floating upwards.

Warm yellow shades or a light purple are good tissue paper colours for this transparency. You could also choose a cooler colour such as blue, as long as it is not too strong or dark.

This transparency is again a double construction, with a base and separate points. You will need three square sheets, as shown above, for the base. Halve them to receive six triangles (see instructions, p. 13). You will also need six square sheets for the points, using the same pattern size as the base.

— *Folding the base:*

0. Make two preparation folds on the six triangles as shown. Unfold.

1. Fold and glue both flaps as shown.

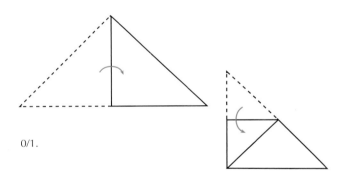

0/1.

0/2.

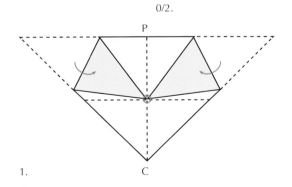

1.

2–3–4. Continue folding as shown.

5. Do a so-called 'sliding fold.' Slide the inner edges onto the outer edges (see arrows). Glue the four marked points. The six base sheets are now finished.

→ Folding the points:

Continue by folding the six points.

6–7. Make a diagonal fold-line and continue folding as shown.

8. Do another 'sliding fold.' Slide the inner edges onto the outer edges (see arrows). Glue. You can also glue the entire inner edge of the folds with a strip of glue.

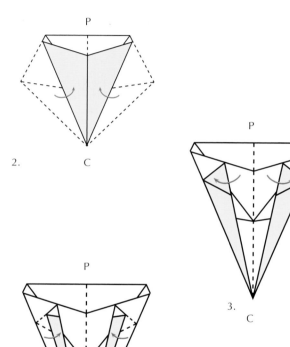

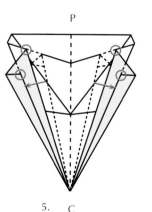

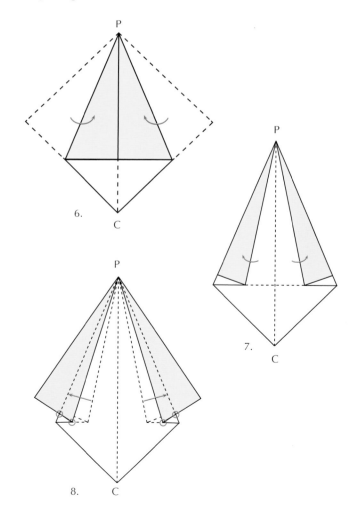

9. Fold as shown.

10. Make a preparation fold at the centre (C). Unfold.

11. Fold out and flatten the middle flaps as shown until their lower corners meet the corners of the orientation fold-line and diagonal, at the same time holding the folds closed at the centre (C) with your forefinger.

12. Now fold two preparation folds on both outer edges. Fold back the centre (C) and glue the four marked points.

13. To finish, fold and glue the side corners.

— *Assembling:*

There are two ways of assembling. Either stick the six base sheets together using the diagram for a six-pointed star (see basic instructions, p. 18) and then glue the points on afterwards. Or glue each point to a base sheet separately before sticking the transparency together using the diagram. In *both* cases it is necessary to *first* glue the lower short orientation line of each point to the upper horizontal edge of the base (red dotted line in the figure), and only then strengthen the transparency by gluing the other marked point.

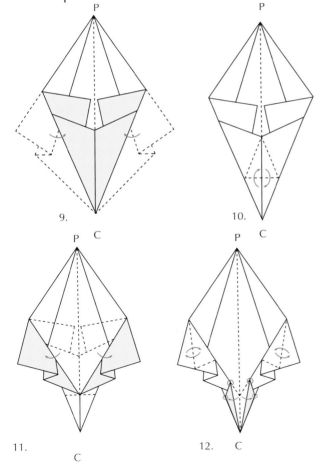

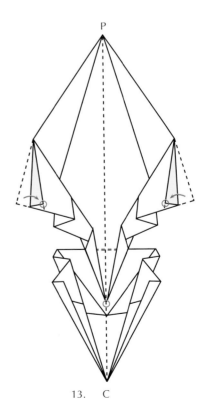

75

15. Cornflower * * * *

EIGHT-POINTED

ø 16³/₄", 42 cm, petals, Pattern 9
flower centre, Pattern 12

This flower transparency is reminiscent of the airy, light-blue summer flowers that are sometimes seen along the edge of a cornfield. The small sections around the centre of the flower are particularly decorative.

This transparency is another double construction, developed out of the previous 'engraved star' transparency. The composition allows one size only, given above.

Use pale pink tissue paper for the flower centre and light blue for the petals. If you want to make the colours more airy, place a large light blue tissue paper sheet over a delicate purple sheet and wet them both well. You can simply sprinkle drops of water onto the pink flower centre (see instructions, p. 11).

Folding the base:

You will need four square sheets for the flower centre, following Pattern 12. Halve them to obtain eight triangles (see instructions, p. 13).

Start with Figures 1–3 of the previous transparency 'engraved star' (p. 73f).

1. Fold the inner edges to the centre fold-line.

2. Do a 'sliding fold' by sliding the inner edges outwards onto the outer edges. Glue the two marked points, the base pieces are now finished.

Folding the petals:

Cut eight squared sheets, Pattern 9, and fold following Figures 6–12 of 'engraved star' (p. 74). Please note that in Figure 8 you do not need the two inner gluing points.

Now turn the sheet so that the point (P) becomes the centre (C) and vice versa.

3. Fold and glue the four side edges.

Assembling:

4. Start with the base. Put the pieces together so that the left edge of the second sheet is glued just beside the right orientation line of the previous sheet, as shown. If you wetted the paper before cutting the sheets out, it is better to leave a tiny gap, hardly $1/32''$ (1 mm), between the two lines. Place your hand over the sheets so that they remain completely flat while gluing. Then push the centre of each petal into the base until it touches the outer edges. Glue. Also glue the side meeting points of the flower petals.

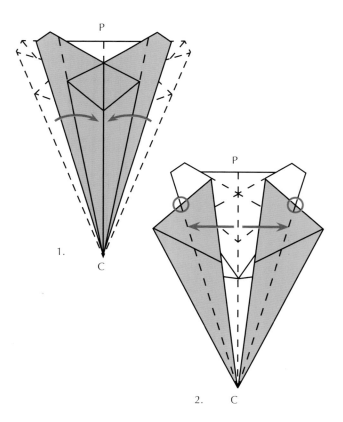

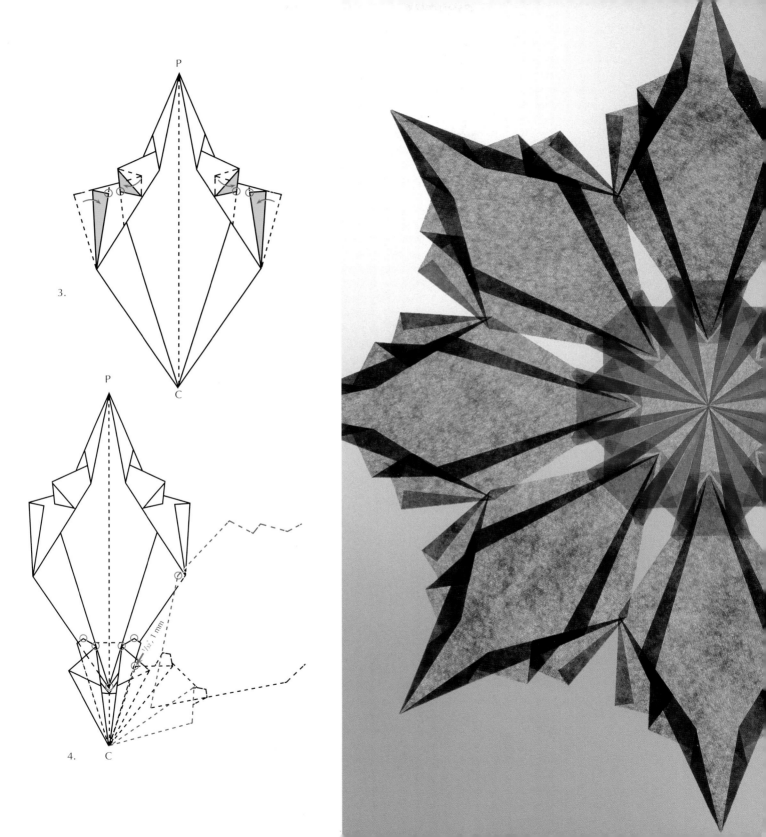

P

C

3.

P

1/32", 1 mm

4. C

16. Auricula flowers * *

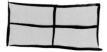

ø 14³/₄", 36.6 cm, Pattern 3
ø 10¹/₂", 26.2 cm, Pattern 2
ø 7¹/₄", 18.2 cm, Pattern 1

The slightly rounded form of this flower brings back memories of the much-loved garden primrose. The special emphasis of this flower lies in the central circle which is clearly differentiated from the rest by its colours. Decorative heralds of spring made out of tissue paper!

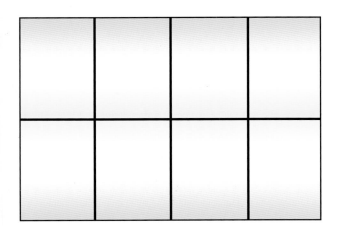

You can imitate the natural play of colours by working on the large uncut sheet of tissue paper (see sketch). The centre circle should be white or light-coloured. Take any light-coloured tissue paper and de-colour the centre with a wet sponge (about less than ¹/₂", 1 cm, for Pattern 1, a bit more, 1.5 cm, for Pattern 2 and ³/₄", 2 cm, for Pattern 3). For a stronger contrast you can paint the rest of the tissue paper with the same shade of watercolour.

Or you can take a white sheet of paper and paint the outer edges a strong colour (e.g. dark yellow) and the inside a lighter colour (e.g. lemon yellow).

Cut five or six rectangular sheets following the pattern above and fold the two centre fold-lines.

1. Fold and glue opposite corners to the centre as shown.

2. Repeat with the remaining two corners.

3. Preparation folds: Fold the two edges to the centre point as shown. Unfold.

4. Now make a so-called 'trumpet fold.' Lift the right lower fold straight up and push the right edge down with your forefinger so that it lies directly above the horizontal orientation fold-line (blue dotted line). Make sure the lower layers do not slip. Do the same folding process for the upper right edge.

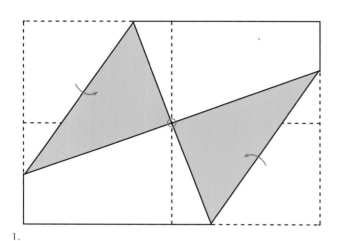

1.

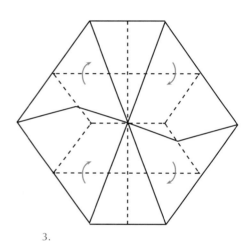

3.

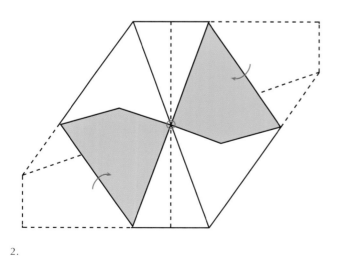

2.

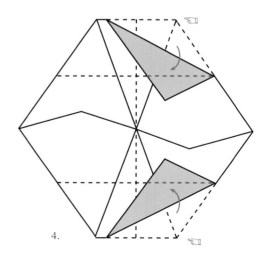

4.

5. Repeat the 'trumpet fold' for the two left edges. Glue the four marked points. The left corner is now the centre (C).

To assemble, use the diagram for five- or six-pointed stars, depending on the amount of sheets you have (see instructions, p. 18). Be careful not to mix up the centre (C) and the point (P) when gluing together, otherwise the transparency will look disproportional!

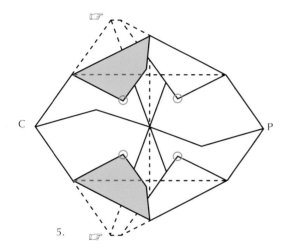

5.

17. Flowering star * *

FIVE-POINTED

ø 14³/₄", 36.6 cm, Pattern 3
ø 10¹/₂", 26.2 cm, Pattern 2
ø 7¹/₄", 18.2 cm, Pattern 1

This flower with its crystalline structure looks like it could bloom forever.

Ice blue, straw yellow or pale pink coloured tissue paper lets the small inner blossom look best. The delicate inner circle will also appear most effectively.

You can easily de-colour the tissue paper with a small sponge to achieve a finely marbled effect. If the colour is left in its natural state the contrasts are also strong.

Cut five rectangular sheets following Patterns 1, 2 or 3.

1. Fold the two centre fold-lines. Fold and glue the upper corners to the centre point.

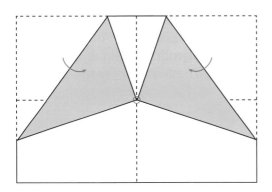

1.

2. Repeat for the two lower corners. Use very little glue.

3. Two preparation folds: fold the lower and upper edges to the centre point. Unfold.

4–5. Now make a 'trumpet fold,' following the same folding process as described for the 'auricula flower' (p. 82), but not in the same sequence, see figure. The centre (C) is at the bottom.

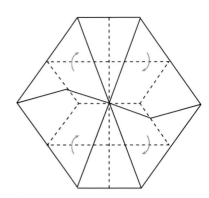

3.

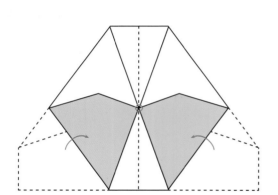

2.

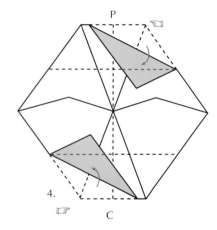

4.

C

6. Bend the four corners back to their outer edges.

7. Fold these edges back inwards. Fold the inner corners downwards so that their base edge makes a horizontal line. Glue the ten marked points.

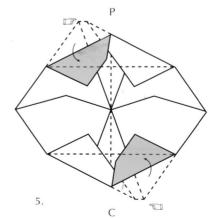

5.

C

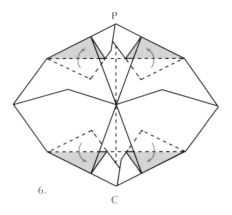

6.

Use the five-pointed diagram to assemble the transparency (see basic instructions, p. 18). While assembling, make sure the inner corners are pointing downwards.

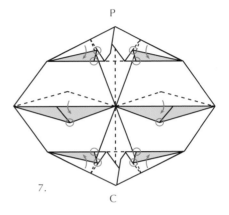

7.

18. Thorn flower * * *

Six-Pointed

ø 16", 40 cm, Pattern 3
ø 11 1/2", 29 cm, Pattern 2
ø 8", 20 cm, Pattern 1

Lots of small, clear arrows define and enliven the slightly circling movements of this transparency. These thorn motifs also convey the impression of an opening bud.

Any light-coloured tissue paper suits this distinct transparency. You can even experiment with light brown on yellow tissue paper and marble them with a wet sponge using little pressure.

The folding technique is a development and continuation of the previous transparency 'flowering star.'

Cut six rectangular sheets following the pattern above and make the two centre fold-lines. Then continue following the instructions for 'flowering star' up to and including Figure 2 (p. 86), *but do not glue the last fold!*

1. Rotate your sheet to suit the figure. Fold the lower preparation fold and unfold. Open up the upper, unglued flaps again.

2. Next, make three 'trumpet folds.' Gently push against the marked outer edges with your forefinger and fold them flat exactly above the orientation line below. While doing this a kind of trumpet form will ensue. Make sure the lower layer of tissue paper does not slip. The newly repositioned edges are a continuation of their respective orientation lines (blue dotted line).

3. Make the last 'trumpet fold' at the right bottom using the same folding process. Fold back the two upper corners as shown.

4. Make the four small arrows by folding back the inner edges to the orientation lines. Do not forget the two preparation folds at the top corners!

5. Fold the last two arrows and glue all the marked points.

Assemble using the six-pointed diagram (see basic instructions, p. 18). Careful, the point (P) and centre (C) have an unusual directional axis, as you can see in the figure.

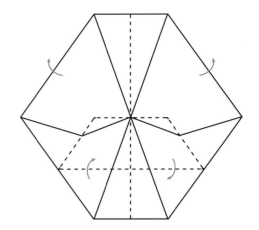

1.

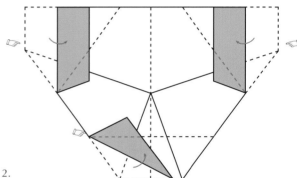

2.

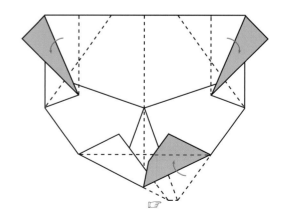

3.

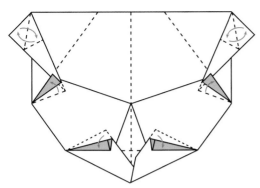

4.

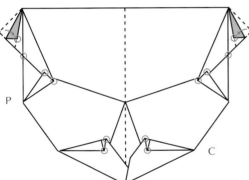

P

5.

C

19. Woven rays * * * *

ø 16", 40 cm, Pattern 16
ø 11", 27.5 cm, Pattern 15

How eight intertwining rays develop into a swirling movement ...

You will need eight rectangular strips to make this airy sun wheel, Pattern 15 or 16.

First make the vertical fold-line by folding the sheet in half and then unfolding.

1. Fold the right side against the centre fold-line. *Turn the sheet over.*

2. Repeat the same fold on the other side. Glue the two left layers of paper at the point marked.

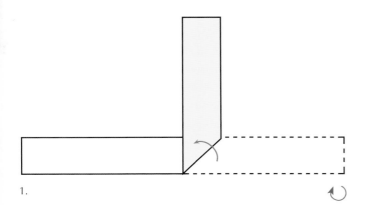

1.

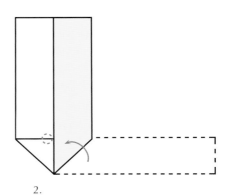

2.

3. Carefully slit open the left diagonal edge to the centre (C) with a razor blade. Fold the now loose edge as shown and glue the three marked points.

At this point you can glue all eight sheets of tissue paper together. *But first turn all the sheets around again, as the newly made folds have to be at the back.* (See basic instructions, p. 16)

4. This figure only shows three sheets glued together. Further secure the transparency by gluing between the two double points (P) as marked. Then fold each right edge to the meeting point of the double edges, tapering towards to the newly glued point. Practical tip: to make this process easier, do not turn the still-fragile transparency but rather turn the plastic film placed under the star before assembling.

5. Fold back the corners. Glue.

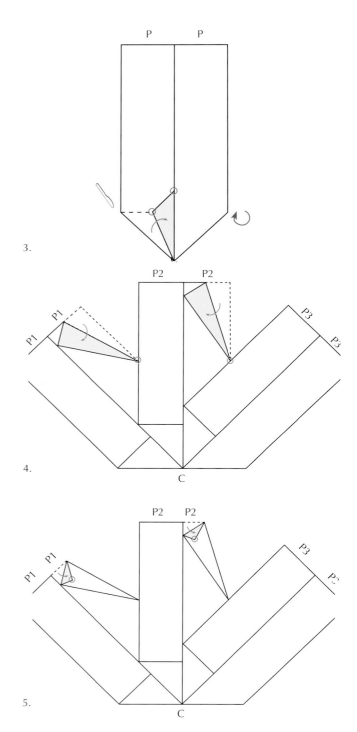

94

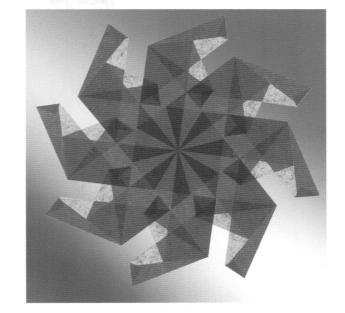

6. Fold the diagonal edge of the folded point (P) towards the centre (C), laying it alongside the neighbouring unfolded part (see blue line). Glue. *Carefully turn the whole transparency over.*

7. Fold the unfolded points (P) to the right along the left edge of the previously folded parts (see blue line).

8. Finish by folding the points (P) as shown in Figures 4 and 5 but using the edges below as a guide line (blue line in figure). The folds should not overlap. Glue the marked points. Finally, strengthen the transparency with strips of glue.

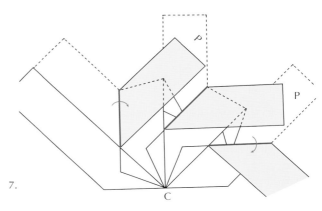

7.

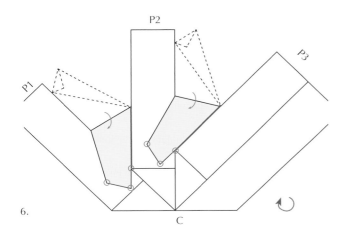

6.

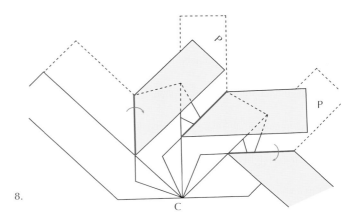

8.

20. Cut crystal * * *

ø 14 ¹/₂", 36 cm, Pattern 2
ø 10 ¹/₂", 26 cm, Pattern 1

A beautifully sculpted snowflake has been blown against the window by the cold winter wind, where it glitters like a star. Precise contours and filigree splinters surround a calm centre. Jewellers art in tissue paper!

Light, cold-coloured tissue paper enhance the different ornamental facets of this transparency. Before cutting the large sheet of tissue paper, you could marble it with drops of water from a wet brush. Or make it two-coloured by irregularly wetting two different coloured sheets of tissue paper placed on top of each other, e.g. pink on blue. Then use the stronger (blue) colour for the outer six points and the lighter (pink) colour for the six-sided base inside (see instructions, p. 11).

Cut twelve rectangular sheets following either Pattern 1 or 2 and make the vertical centre fold-line. Unfold. Fold the horizontal centre fold-line. But do not unfold again! Leave the sheet doubled until Figure 7.

1. Fold down the two edges of the upper layer as shown, the point of the diagonal edges exactly on the centre fold-line.

2–3. Fold as shown.

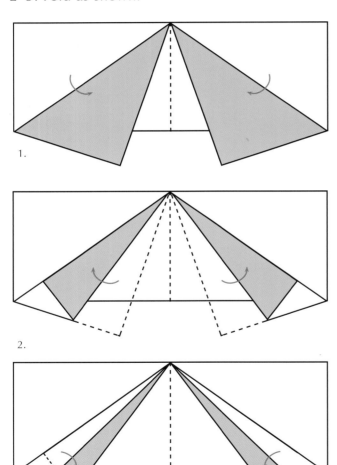

4. Fold and glue the two tiny corners, *without gluing the lower layer.*

5–6. Proceed as shown. Glue. *Turn the sheet around and repeat the folding process 1–6 on the other side.*

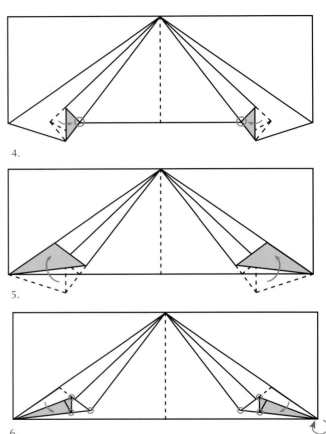

7. Unfold the sheet. Make the preparation fold at the centre (C) by folding its point to the centre fold-line. Unfold.

8. Take the six sheets intended for the base and glue the side flaps to the newly made meeting point of the fold-lines.

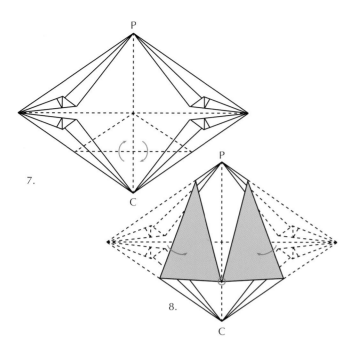

7.

8.

orientation point. Glue the two marked points. To finish, strengthen the transparency with strips of glue.

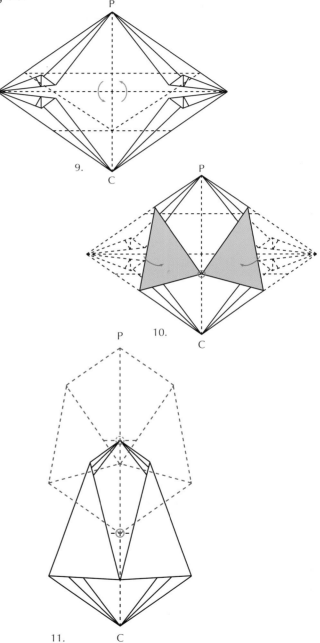

9.

10.

11.

— *Assembling the six base pieces:*

Use the six-pointed diagram to glue the base together (see basic instructions, p. 18).

— *Folding the six points:*

9. Make a new preparation fold on the remaining six sheets. Fold the point (P) to the lower meeting point of the orientation lines and unfold. *Now turn the sheet around so that the point (P) becomes the centre (C) and vice versa.*

10. Glue the side flaps to the newly made fold-line meeting point.

11. Glue the six points to the crystal base. *Make sure you do not mix up (P) and (C) whilst gluing together!* The centre (C) is at the wider end. Use both meeting points of the centre fold-lines as an

21. Chrysanthemum * * *

SIXTEEN-POINTED

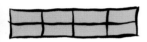

ø 20", 50 cm,
Pattern 16

ø 13 1/3", 34 cm,
Pattern 15

This airy flower with its great winged petals is reminiscent of a large Japanese chrysanthemum. Its light elegance is revealed like a peaceful garden atmosphere before the autumn winds can blow away the finely structured petals.

Cut sixteen rectangular strips of tissue paper following Pattern 15 or 16. Fold the horizontal centre fold-lines first and then fold twice vertically for three short vertical orientation folds. Make all folds crisp before unfolding to ensure they remain clear (see small sketch above).

1–4. Fold as shown at *both ends*. Use the back of a knife to make both (C/P) points perfect. Then glue the marked points.

5. Bend the (C) or (P) point to the left along the short inner edge (red line). Glue. Turn the sheet to make the same fold on the other side. The points are folded mirror images of each other.

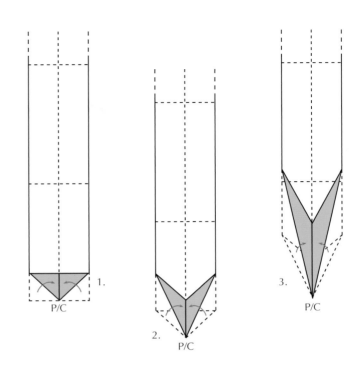

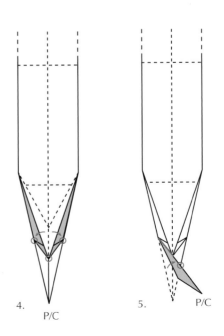

6. Fold the sheets in half along the centre fold. Now fold the new end of the sheet, which is the centre (C), following Figures 1 and 2. The sheet looks like a fish at this stage. Fold the left (C) side only following Figures 3–5. Now fold the upper point (P1) down to the right, its left edge aligned with the first horizontal fold-line. Glue the three marked points. Figure 6 only shows the finished product of the whole folding process.

7. First glue the sixteen finished points together in pairs. You will have eight pairs, overlapping so that the left (C) edge of the second sheet is glued to the inner edge of the first sheet (shown by the red line).

Fold the concealed point (P1) forwards over the other. Glue the other marked points.

Make a preparation fold at the centre (C) by folding the point back straight along the right edge as shown. Unfold.

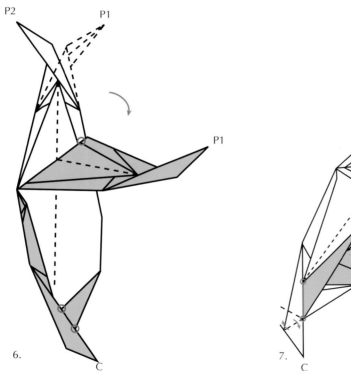

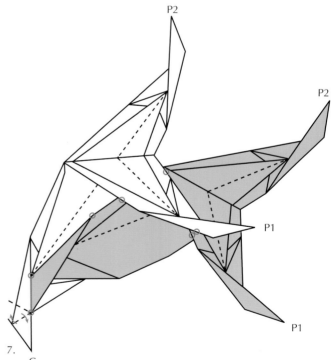

8. The principle of gluing these eight pairs together is the same as assembling an eight-pointed star (see basic instructions, p. 16).

The figure shows the outlines of two assembled pairs. The left wide angle at the corner of the newly made fold-line has now become *the new centre (C)*. The grey shaded area clarifies where the two sheets overlap.

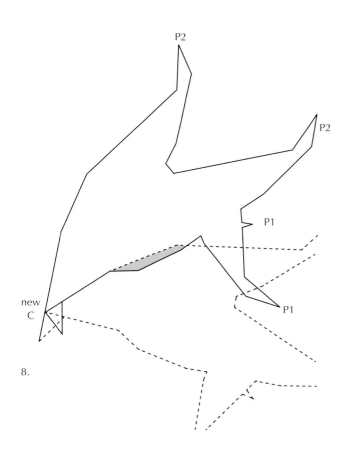

P2

P2

P1

P1

new
C

8.

22. Sun heart * * * *

EIGHT-POINTED

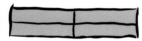

ø 20", 50 cm, Pattern 16
ø 14", 35 cm, Pattern 15

The light and dark dynamic of this transparency is enhanced by opposing movements of the inner and outer rays. Pulsating solar energy in the sky!

Cut eight long rectangular pieces following Pattern 15 or 16. Make both centre fold-lines very crisp so these orientation lines remain clear.

1–2. The first steps are the same as 'woven rays' (p. 93). *Do not forget to turn the sheet over after Figure 1!* The left gluing point is important.

3. Fold the inner edge of the point (P2) to the right to lie along the lower outer diagonal edge.

4. Carefully slit open the left diagonal edge to the centre (C). Glue the centre point immediately and then continue folding as shown. Glue the second marked point.

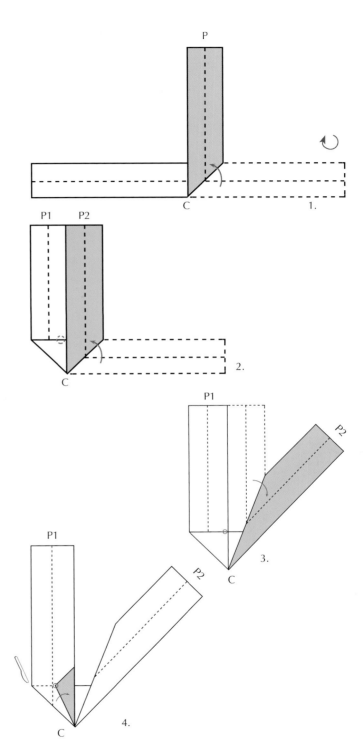

105

5. Now assemble all eight sheets (see basic instructions, p. 16). In this exceptional case pairs of sheets are placed over each other. The figure shows three pairs glued together.

This process should be done very carefully, using a plastic film underneath to turn the transparency (as described for the 'woven rays') to ensure the pairs stay exactly on top of each other.

Then fold the loose corners in the centre area to the left to meet the centre fold-line. Glue.

Fold back the upper strip (P1) until the lower edge hits the meeting point of the two strips and the left edge reaches to the edge of the concealed strip (P2) seen through the tissue paper (shown by the blue dots).

6. Fold down the corners of the upper strip (P1) to the edge of the concealed strip (P2).

7. Fold these strips (P1) down towards the centre as shown clearly. Glue. Now fold the other strips (P2). Glue.

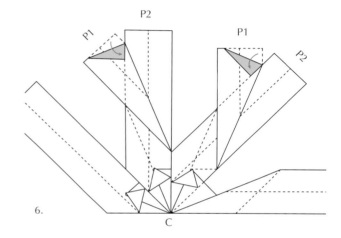

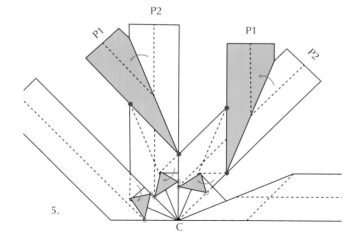

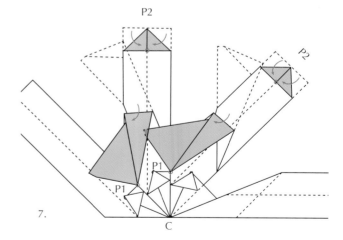

8–9. Finish folding and glue the strips (P2). To finish, glue dots or strips of glue where necessary to strengthen the sun structure.

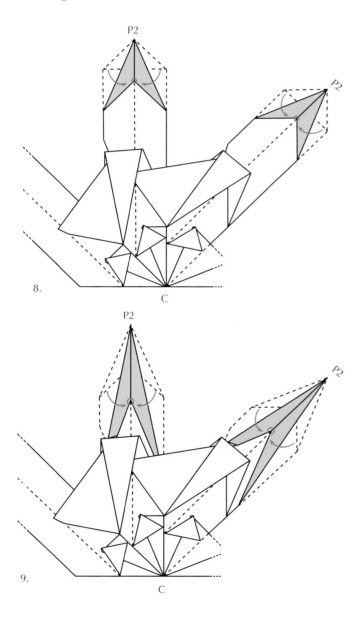

8.

9.

23. Wind wheel * * *

SIXTEEN-POINTED

ø 18 $\frac{1}{4}$", 45.5 cm,
Pattern 16

ø 12 $\frac{3}{4}$", 32 cm,
Pattern 15

This slowly turning wheel motif stimulates the observer's imagination. Depending on the chosen colour the wheel can be experienced either as warmth, air or water.

A warm tissue paper colour will give the impression of a sun wheel, a cooler colour of a waterwheel or a windmill. The colour should not be too dark to let the rolling energy remain visible.

Cut eight rectangular strips, following Pattern 15 or 16. *Halve these sheets* to obtain 16 strips Pattern 15: 7" (17.5 cm) long and 1 $\frac{1}{3}$" (4.16 cm) wide; Pattern 16: 10" (25 cm) long, 2 $\frac{1}{3}$" (5.8 cm) wide. Make the centre fold-line along the length.

1–3. Fold the point (P) as shown and glue. *Turn the sheet over!*

4. Continue folding as shown.

5. Now fold the twist: Hold the centre (C) with your right hand and bend the point (P) up and around to the right with your left hand as shown. If you place a thin ruler diagonally across these two points (•) you can fold quickly and accurately.

To achieve an even and thus harmoniously rotating wind wheel it is advisable to make sure the right hand edge is the same length on all sheets (see arrows), and if necessary to adjust the folds. Only then glue the marked point.

6. Fold and glue the centre (C).

Assemble this sixteen-pointed transparency the same as an eight-pointed transparency (see basic instructions, p. 17). Because the sheets are not very stable it is necessary to stick the centre part with long strips of glue.

Before sticking the wind wheel (sun wheel) to the window you will need to stick short lengths of adhesive tape behind each point. Fasten the wind wheel to the window by starting at the centre and spreading the points out evenly in a circle.

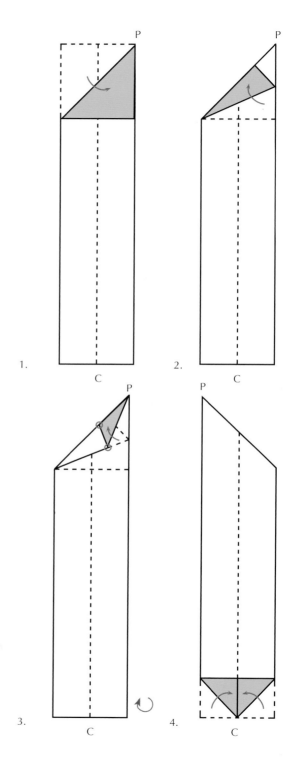

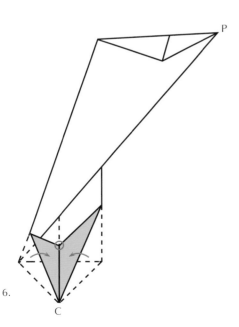

5.

1.9', 4.8 cm, Pattern 15
2.9', 7.3 cm, Pattern 16

P

C

6.

P

C

24. Evening sun * * * *

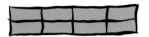

ø 17 ½", 43.5 cm,
Pattern 7

This setting sun still stands triumphantly over the horizon at the end of a hot summer's day. Majestic and picturesque she descends slowly and peacefully in a blaze of colour.

Choose two matching tissue paper colours to support the swirling movement. Pale pink for the inner rays and a gentle yellow for the outer rays look good. This sun is most impressive if you enliven the tissue paper by wetting it before cutting the small sheets. Do this by sandwiching half a yellow sheet of tissue paper between a large doubled pink sheet and liberally and randomly wetting both with a sponge in lots of different places. You can repeat this process on the other side too (see instructions, p. 11).

You will need a whole sheet of tissue paper for the outer rays, but only half a sheet for the inner rays:, making a total of 24 long strips following Pattern 7. Fold in half and fold in half again, smoothing down the folds to make crisp lines, and unfold. You will have three clear short foldlines on each strip.

Take the eight small strips (from the half sheet) intended for the inner rays of the centre. Halve these sheets with a knife to make 16 shorter rectangular pieces; size: 7" × 2 ½" (17.5 cm × 6.25 cm).

Make a horizontal centre fold for all 32 sheets (16 long sheets for the outer rays and 16 short sheets for the inner rays).

The 16 long outer rays:

1. Fold the right lower edge to the next vertical fold-line. *Turn the sheet over.*

2. Fold the longer half of the sheet upwards to the same vertical fold-line. *Turn the sheet over again.*

The sixteen short inner rays:

3. Take the shorter sheets and fold as shown.

4. Now pair a short and a long sheet together by pushing the short sheet into the long sheet as shown: centre to centre point and left edge placed on the centre fold-line of the long sheet. The right lower part of the short sheet is concealed by the longer sheet. Glue the three marked points.

5. Three preparation folds: fold the three corners to their respective right edges and unfold.

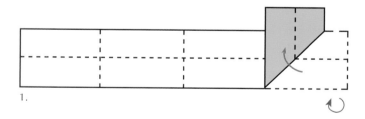

1.

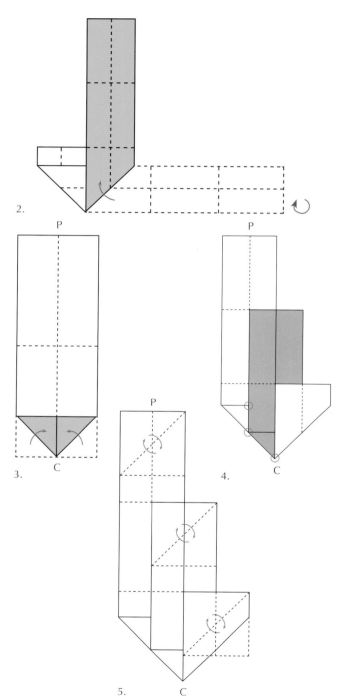

2.

3.   P   C

4.   P   C

5.   P   C

6–7. Fold as shown. Then glue the eight marked points. Carefully slit the long left edge, shown in red, with a razor blade.

8. First fold out the right part. Make the two small folds as shown in Figures 6 and 7. Glue the four marked points.

9. Fold the right part back so that its outer point can be glued to the centre fold-line. Now fold the next point downwards and glue it to the same point.

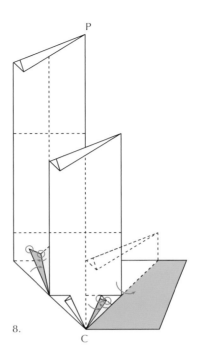

8.

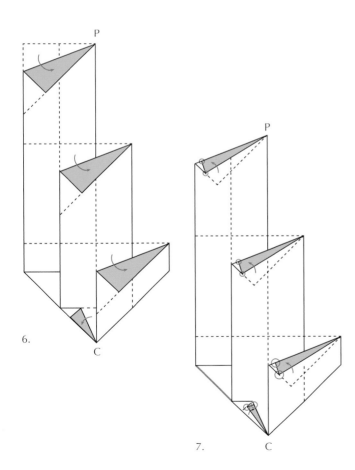

6.

7.

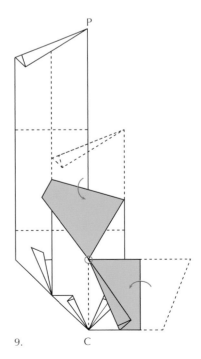

9.

115

10. Before folding the uppermost point (P) as shown you will need to find the necessary orientation point. To do this, make the small preparation fold with the central left corner as shown. Place the point (P) exactly on this point. Then unfold the small corner and glue the two marked points. *Turn the sheet over!*

11. Slit the whole lower left edge open with a razor blade (red line). Glue the left corner. Fold the top layer of paper of the newly opened corner up to the lower diagonal edge seen through the tissue paper.

12. Finish the last fold. Fold back the left small corner of the lower layer of paper. Glue the marked points. *Turn the sheet back over.*

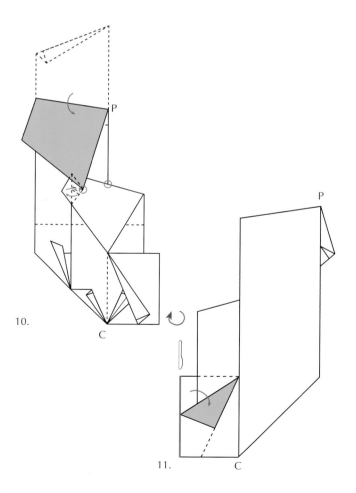

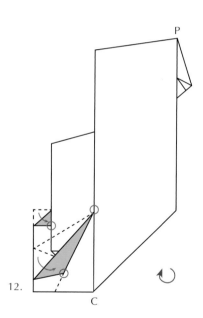

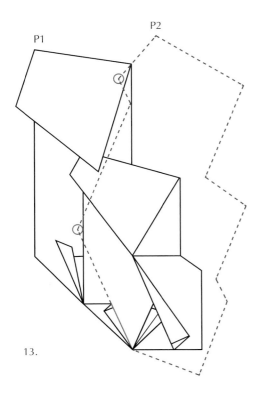

P1   P2

13.

━ *Assembling the sixteen sheets:*

13. Place the second sheet onto the inner left (C) diagonal edge of the first sheet (red line) as shown. Place your hand over the whole sheet so that the layers of tissue paper remain flat while gluing. Strengthen the transparency with additional strips of glue.

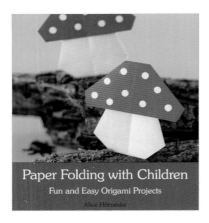

Paper Folding with Children

Fun and Easy Origami Projects

Alice Hörnecke

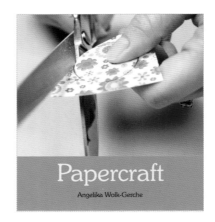

Papercraft

Angelika Wolk-Gerche

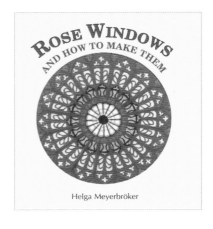

ROSE WINDOWS
AND HOW TO MAKE THEM

Helga Meyerbröker

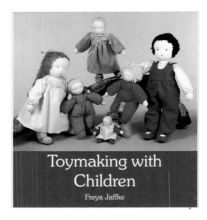

Toymaking with Children

Freya Jaffke

Feltcraft

Making Dolls, Gifts and Toys

Petra Berger

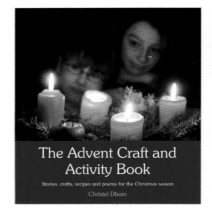

The Advent Craft and Activity Book

Stories, crafts, recipes and poems for the Christmas season

Christel Dhom

Magic Wool

Creative Pictures and Tableaux with Natural Sheep's Wool

Freya Jaffke and Dagmar Schmidt

Crafts Through the Year

Thomas and Petra Berger

Magic Wool Fairies

Christine Schäfer

florisbooks.co.uk